FOREWORD

The collection of "Everything Will Be Okay" travel phrasebooks published by T&P Books is designed for people traveling abroad for tourism and business. The phrasebooks contain what matters most - the essentials for basic communication. This is an indispensable set of phrases to "survive" while abroad.

This phrasebook will help you in most cases where you need to ask something, get directions, find out how much something costs, etc. It can also resolve difficult communication situations where gestures just won't help.

This book contains a lot of phrases that have been grouped according to the most relevant topics. A separate section of the book also provides a small dictionary with more than 1,500 important and useful words.

Take "Everything Will Be Okay" phrasebook with you on the road and you'll have an irreplaceable traveling companion who will help you find your way out of any situation and teach you to not fear speaking with foreigners.

TABLE OF CONTENTS

T&P Books Publishing

PHRASEBOOK

— ARABIC —

THE MOST IMPORTANT PHRASES

This phrasebook contains
the most important
phrases and questions
for basic communication
Everything you need
to survive overseas

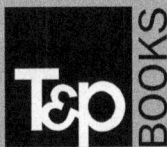

By Andrey Taranov

T&P BOOKS

Phrasebook + 1500-word dictionary

English-Arabic phrasebook & concise dictionary

By Andrey Taranov

The collection of "Everything Will Be Okay" travel phrasebooks published by T&P Books is designed for people traveling abroad for tourism and business. The phrasebooks contain what matters most - the essentials for basic communication. This is an indispensable set of phrases to "survive" while abroad.

Another section of the book also provides a small dictionary with more than 1,500 useful words arranged alphabetically. The dictionary includes a lot of gastronomic terms and will be helpful when ordering food at a restaurant or buying groceries at the store.

T&P Books Publishing
www.tpbooks.com

ISBN: 978-1-78716-927-2

This book is also available in E-book formats.
Please visit www.tpbooks.com or the major online bookstores.

PRONUNCIATION

T&P phonetic alphabet	Arabic example	English example
[a]	طَفَّى [ṭaffa]	shorter than in ask
[ā]	إختار [iχtār]	calf, palm
[e]	هامبورجر [hamburger]	elm, medal
[i]	زفاف [zifāf]	shorter than in feet
[ī]	أبريل [abrīl]	feet, meter
[u]	كلكتا [kalkutta]	book
[ū]	جاموس [ʒāmūs]	fuel, tuna
[b]	بداية [bidāya]	baby, book
[d]	سعادة [saʿāda]	day, doctor
[ḍ]	وضع [waḍʿ]	[d] pharyngeal
[ʒ]	الأرجنتين [arʒantīn]	forge, pleasure
[ð]	تذكار [tiðkār]	pharyngealized th
[ẓ]	ظهر [ẓahar]	[z] pharyngeal
[f]	خفيف [χafīf]	face, food
[g]	جولف [gūlf]	game, gold
[h]	إتّجاه [ittiʒāh]	home, have
[ḥ]	أحبّ [aḥabb]	[h] pharyngeal
[y]	ذهبيّ [ðahabiy]	yes, New York
[k]	كرسيّ [kursiy]	clock, kiss
[l]	لمح [lamaḥ]	lace, people
[m]	مرصد [marṣad]	magic, milk
[n]	جنوب [ʒanūb]	sang, thing
[p]	كابتشينو [kaputʃīnu]	pencil, private
[q]	وثق [waθiq]	king, club
[r]	روح [rūḥ]	rice, radio
[s]	سخريّة [suχriyya]	city, boss
[ṣ]	معصم [miʿṣam]	[s] pharyngeal
[ʃ]	عشاء [ʿaʃāʾ]	machine, shark
[t]	تنّوب [tannūb]	tourist, trip
[ṭ]	خريطة [χarīṭa]	[t] pharyngeal
[θ]	ماموث [mamūθ]	month, tooth
[v]	فيتنام [vitnām]	very, river
[w]	ودّع [waddaʿ]	vase, winter
[χ]	بخيل [baχīl]	as in Scots 'loch'
[ɣ]	تغدّى [taɣadda]	between [g] and [h]
[z]	ماعز [māʿiz]	zebra, please

T&P phonetic alphabet	Arabic example	English example
['] (ayn)	[sab'a] سبعة	voiced pharyngeal fricative
['] (hamza)	[sa'al] سأل	glottal stop

LIST OF ABBREVIATIONS

Arabic abbreviations

du	-	plural noun (double)
f	-	feminine noun
m	-	masculine noun
pl	-	plural

English abbreviations

ab.	-	about
adj	-	adjective
adv	-	adverb
anim.	-	animate
as adj	-	attributive noun used as adjective
e.g.	-	for example
etc.	-	et cetera
fam.	-	familiar
fem.	-	feminine
form.	-	formal
inanim.	-	inanimate
masc.	-	masculine
math	-	mathematics
mil.	-	military
n	-	noun
pl	-	plural
pron.	-	pronoun
sb	-	somebody
sing.	-	singular
sth	-	something
v aux	-	auxiliary verb
vi	-	intransitive verb
vi, vt	-	intransitive, transitive verb
vt	-	transitive verb

T&P BOOKS

ARABIC
PHRASEBOOK

This section contains
important phrases that may
come in handy in various
real-life situations.
The phrasebook will help
you ask for directions, clarify
a price, buy tickets, and
order food at a restaurant

T&P Books Publishing

PHRASEBOOK
CONTENTS

T&P Books Publishing

The bare minimum

Excuse me, ...	ba'd ezznak, ... ،بعد إذنك
Hello.	ahlan أهلاً
Thank you.	ʃokran شكراً
Good bye.	ella alliqā' إلى اللقاء
Yes.	aywā أيوة
No.	la'a لأ
I don't know.	ma'raʃʃ ما أعرفش
Where? | Where to? | When?	feyn? | lefeyn? | emta? إمتى؟ ا لفين؟ ا فين؟

I need ...	mehtāg ... ... ممتاج
I want ...	'āyez ... ... عايز
Do you have ...?	ya tara 'andak ...? يا ترى عندك... ؟
Is there a ... here?	feyh hena ...? فيه هنا ...؟
May I ...?	momken ...? ممكن ...؟
..., please (polite request)	... men faḍlak ... من فضلك

I'm looking for ...	ana badawwar 'la ... ... أنا بادور على
restroom	hammām حمام
ATM	makīnet ṣarraf 'āaly ماكينة صراف آلي
pharmacy (drugstore)	ṣaydaliya صيدلية
hospital	mostaʃfa مستشفى
police station	'essm el ʃorṭa قسم شرطة
subway	metro el anfā' مترو الأنفاق

taxi	taksi تاكسي
train station	mahattet el 'attr محطة القطر

My name is ...	essmy ... إسمي...
What's your name?	essmak eyh? اسمك إيه؟
Could you please help me?	te'ddar tesā'dny? تقدر تساعدني؟
I've got a problem.	ana 'andy moʃkela أنا عندي مشكلة
I don't feel well.	ana ta'bān أنا تعبان
Call an ambulance!	otlob 'arabeyet es'āf! أطلب عربية إسعاف!
May I make a call?	momken a'mel mokalma telefoniya? ممكن أعمل مكالمة تليفونية؟

I'm sorry.	ana 'āssif أنا آسف
You're welcome.	el 'afw العفو

I, me	ana أنا
you (inform.)	enta أنت
he	howwa هو
she	hiya هي
they (masc.)	homm هم
they (fem.)	homm هم
we	ehna احنا
you (pl)	entom انتم
you (sg, form.)	haddretak حضرتك

ENTRANCE	doχūl دخول
EXIT	χorūg خروج
OUT OF ORDER	'attlān عطلان
CLOSED	moγlaq مغلق

OPEN	maftūḥ
	مفتوح
FOR WOMEN	lel sayedāt
	للسيدات
FOR MEN	lel regāl
	للرجال

Questions

Where?	feyn? فين؟
Where to?	lefeyn? لفين؟
Where from?	men feyn? من فين؟
Why?	leyh? ليه؟
For what reason?	le'ayī sabab? لأي سبب؟
When?	emta? إمتى؟
How long?	leḥadd emta? لحد إمتى؟
At what time?	fi ayī sā'a? في أي ساعة؟
How much?	bekām? بكام؟
Do you have ...?	ya tara 'andak ...? يا ترى عندك ...؟
Where is ...?	feyn ...? فين ...؟
What time is it?	el sā'a kām? الساعة كام؟
May I make a call?	momken a'mel mokalma telefoniya? ممكن أعمل مكالمة تليفونية؟
Who's there?	meyn henāk? مين هناك؟
Can I smoke here?	momken addaxen hena? ممكن أدخن هنا؟
May I ...?	momken ...? ممكن ...؟

Needs

I'd like ...	aḥebb ... أحب ...
I don't want ...	meʃ ʿāyiz ... مش عايز ...
I'm thirsty.	ana ʿaṭʃān أنا عطشان
I want to sleep.	ʿāyez anām عايز أنام

I want ...	ʿāyez ... عايز ...
to wash up	atʃaṭṭaf أتشطف
to brush my teeth	aɣsel senāny أغسل سناني
to rest a while	artāḥ ʃwaya أرتاح شوية
to change my clothes	aɣayar hodūmy أغير هدومي

to go back to the hotel	argaʿ lel fondoq أرجع للفندق
to buy ...	ʃerāʾ ... شراء ...
to go to ...	arūḥ le... أروح لـ...
to visit ...	azūr ... أزور ...
to meet with ...	aʿābel ... أقابل ...
to make a call	aʿmel mokalma telefoniya أعمل مكالمة تليفونية

I'm tired.	ana taʿbān أنا تعبان
We are tired.	eḥna taʿbānīn إحنا تعبانين
I'm cold.	ana bardān أنا بردان
I'm hot.	ana ḥarran أنا حران
I'm OK.	ana kowayes أنا كويس

I need to make a call.	mehtāg aʿmel mokalma telefoneya محتاج أعمل مكالمة تليفونية
I need to go to the restroom.	mehtāg arūh el ḥammam محتاج أروح الحمام
I have to go.	lāzem amʃy لازم أمشي
I have to go now.	lāzem amʃy dellwa'ty لازم أمشي دلوقتي

Asking for directions

Excuse me, ...	ba'd ezznak, ... بعد إذنك، ...
Where is ...?	feyn ...? فين ...؟
Which way is ...?	meneyn ...? منين ...؟
Could you help me, please?	momken tesā'edny, men faḍlak? ممكن تساعدني، من فضلك؟
I'm looking for ...	ana badawwar 'la ... أنا بادور على ...
I'm looking for the exit.	baddawwar 'la ṭarīq el xorūg بادور على طريق الخروج
I'm going to ...	ana rāyeḥ le... أنا رايح لـ...
Am I going the right way to ...?	ana māʃy fel ṭarīq el saḥḥ le ...? أنا ماشي في الطريق الصح لـ... ؟
Is it far?	howwa be'īd? هو بعيد؟
Can I get there on foot?	momken awṣal henāk māʃy? ممكن أوصل هناك ماشي؟
Can you show me on the map?	momken tewarrīny 'lal xarīṭa? ممكن توريني على الخريطة؟
Show me where we are right now.	momken tewarrīny eḥna feyn dellwa'ty? ممكن توريني إحنا فين دلوقتي؟
Here	hena هنا
There	henāk هناك
This way	men hena من هنا
Turn right.	oddxol yemīn ادخل يمين
Turn left.	oddxol ʃemal ادخل شمال
first (second, third) turn	awwel (tāny, tālet) ʃāre' أول (تاني، تالت) شارع

to the right	'lal yemīn على اليمين
to the left	'lal ʃemal على الشمال
Go straight ahead.	'la ṭūl على طول

Signs

WELCOME!	marḥaba
	مرحبا
ENTRANCE	doχūl
	دخول
EXIT	χorūg
	خروج

PUSH	eddfaʿ
	إدفع
PULL	ess-ḥab
	إسحب
OPEN	maftūḥ
	مفتوح
CLOSED	moγlaq
	مغلق

FOR WOMEN	lel sayedāt
	للسيدات
FOR MEN	lel regāl
	للرجال
GENTLEMEN, GENTS (m)	el sāda
	السادة
WOMEN (f)	el sayedāt
	السيدات

DISCOUNTS	taχfīḍāt
	تخفيضات
SALE	okazyōn
	اوكازيون
FREE	maggānan
	مجانا
NEW!	gedīd!
	!جديد
ATTENTION!	ennttabeh!
	!إنتبه

NO VACANCIES	mafīʃ makān
	ما فيش مكان
RESERVED	maḥgūz
	محجوز
ADMINISTRATION	el edāra
	الإدارة
STAFF ONLY	lel ʿāmelīn faqaṭ
	للعاملين فقط

BEWARE OF THE DOG!	ehhtaress men el kalb! إحترس من الكلب
NO SMOKING!	mammnū' el tadχīn! ممنوع التدخين!
DO NOT TOUCH!	mammnū' el lammss! ممنوع اللمس!
DANGEROUS	χatīr خطير
DANGER	χatar خطر
HIGH VOLTAGE	gohd 'āly جهد عالي
NO SWIMMING!	mammnū' el sebāḥa! ممنوع السباحة!

OUT OF ORDER	'aṭlān عطلان
FLAMMABLE	qābel lel efte'āl قابل للإشتعال
FORBIDDEN	mammnū' ممنوع
NO TRESPASSING!	mammnū' el taχaṭṭy! ممنوع التخطي!
WET PAINT	ṭalā' ḥadiis طلاء حديث

CLOSED FOR RENOVATIONS	moγlaq lel tagdedāt مغلق للتجديدات
WORKS AHEAD	afγāl fel ṭarīq أشغال في الطريق
DETOUR	monḥany منحنى

Transportation. General phrases

plane	ṭayāra طيّارة
train	'attr قطر
bus	otobiis اوتوبيس
ferry	safīna سفينة
taxi	taksi تاكسي
car	'arabiya عربية

schedule	gadwal جدول
Where can I see the schedule?	a'dar aʃūf el gadwal feyn? أقدر أشوف الجدول فين؟
workdays (weekdays)	ayām el ossbū' أيام الأسبوع
weekends	nehāyet el osbū' نهاية الأسبوع
holidays	el 'agazāt الأجازات

DEPARTURE	el saffar السفر
ARRIVAL	el wosūl الوصول
DELAYED	mett'xara متأخرة
CANCELLED	molɣā ملغاه

next (train, etc.)	el gayī الجاي
first	el awwel الأول
last	el 'axīr الأخير

When is the next ...?	emta el ... elly gayī? إللي جاي؟ ... إمتى الـ
When is the first ...?	emta awwel ...? إمتى اول ...؟

When is the last ...?	emta 'āχer ...?
	إمتى آخر ...؟
transfer (change of trains, etc.)	tabdīl
	تبديل
to make a transfer	abaddel
	أبدل
Do I need to make a transfer?	hal ahtāg le tabdīl el...?
	هل أحتاج لتبديل الـ...؟

Buying tickets

Where can I buy tickets?	meneyn momken aʃtery tazāker? منين ممكن أشتري تذاكر؟
ticket	tazzkara تذكرة
to buy a ticket	ʃerā' tazāker شراء تذاكر
ticket price	as'ār el tazāker أسعار التذاكر

Where to?	lefeyn? لفين؟
To what station?	le'ayī maḥaṭṭa? لأي محطة؟
I need ...	meḥtāg ... محتاج ...
one ticket	tazzkara waḥda تذكرة واحدة
two tickets	tazzkarteyn تذكرتين
three tickets	talat tazāker تلات تذاكر

one-way	zehāb faqaṭṭ ذهاب فقط
round-trip	zehāb we 'awda ذهاب وعودة
first class	daraga ūla درجة أولى
second class	daraga tanya درجة ثانية

today	el naharda النهاردة
tomorrow	bokra بكرة
the day after tomorrow	ba'd bokra بعد بكرة
in the morning	el sobḥ الصبح
in the afternoon	ba'd el ẓohr بعد الظهر
in the evening	bel leyl بالليل

aisle seat	korsy mammar كرسي ممر
window seat	korsy ʃebbāk كرسي شباك
How much?	bekām? بكام؟
Can I pay by credit card?	momken addfaʻ be kart eʼtemān? ممكن أدفع بكارت إئتمان؟

Bus

bus	el otobiis
	الأوتوبيس
intercity bus	otobiis beyn el moddon
	أوتوبيس بين المدن
bus stop	mahattet el otobiis
	محطة الأوتوبيس
Where's the nearest bus stop?	feyn aqrab mahattet otobiis?
	فين أقرب محطة أوتوبيس؟
number (bus ~, etc.)	raqam
	رقم
Which bus do I take to get to ...?	'āxod ayī otobiis le ...?
	أخذ أي اوتوبيس لـ...؟
Does this bus go to ...?	el otobiis da beyrūh ...?
	الأوتوبيس دة بيروح ...؟
How frequent are the buses?	el otobiis beyīgi kol 'add eyh?
	الأوتوبيس بيجي كل قد إيه؟
every 15 minutes	kol xamasstāʃar daqīqa
	كل 15 دقيقة
every half hour	kol noss sā'a
	كل نص ساعة
every hour	kol sā'a
	كل ساعة
several times a day	kaza marra fel yome
	كذا مرة في اليوم
... times a day	... marrat fell yome
	مرات في اليوم ...
schedule	gadwal
	جدول
Where can I see the schedule?	a'dar aʃūf el gadwal feyn?
	أقدر أشوف الجدول فين؟
When is the next bus?	emta el otobīss elly gayī?
	إمتى الأتوبيس إللي جاي؟
When is the first bus?	emta awwel otobiis?
	إمتى أول أوتوبيس؟
When is the last bus?	emta 'āxer otobiis?
	إمتى آخر أوتوبيس؟
stop	mahatta
	محطة
next stop	el mahatta el gaya
	المحطة الجاية

last stop (terminus)

axer mahatta
آخر محطة (أخر الخط)

Stop here, please.

laww samaht, wa'eff hena
لو سمحت، وقف هنا

Excuse me, this is my stop.

ba'd ezznak, di mahattetti
بعد إذنك، دي محطتي

Train

train	el 'attr القطر
suburban train	'attr el dawāhy قطر الضواحي
long-distance train	'attr el masāfāt el tawīla قطر المسافات الطويلة
train station	mahattet el 'attr محطة القطر
Excuse me, where is the exit to the platform?	ba'd ezznak, meneyn el tarīq lel rasīf بعد إذنك، منين الطريق للرصيف؟
Does this train go to ...?	el 'attr da beyrūh ...? القطر دة بيروح ...؟
next train	el 'attr el gayī? القطر الجاي؟
When is the next train?	emta el 'attr elly gayī? إمتى القطر إللي جاي؟
Where can I see the schedule?	a'dar aſūf el gadwal feyn? أقدر أشوف الجدول فين؟
From which platform?	men ayī rasīf? من أي رصيف؟
When does the train arrive in ...?	emta yewsal el 'attr ...? إمتى يوصل القطر ... ؟
Please help me.	argūk sā'dny ارجوك ساعدني
I'm looking for my seat.	baddawwar 'lal korsy betā'y بادور على الكرسي بتاعي
We're looking for our seats.	ehna benndawwar 'la karāsy إحنا بندور على كراسي
My seat is taken.	el korsy betā'i maſɣūl الكرسي بتاعي مشغول
Our seats are taken.	karaseyna maſɣūla كراسينا مشغولة
I'm sorry but this is my seat.	'ann ezznak, el korsy da betā'y عن إذنك، الكرسي دة بتاعي
Is this seat taken?	el korsy da mahgūz? الكرسي دة محجوز؟
May I sit here?	momken a''od hena? ممكن أقعد هنا؟

On the train. Dialogue (No ticket)

Ticket, please.	tazāker men faḍlak
	تذاكر من فضلك
I don't have a ticket.	ma'andīʃ tazzkara
	ما عنديش تذكرة
I lost my ticket.	tazzkarty ḍā'et
	تذكرتي ضاعت
I forgot my ticket at home.	nesīt tazkarty fel beyt
	نسيت تذكرتي في البيت
You can buy a ticket from me.	momken teʃtery menny tazkara
	ممكن تشتري مني تذكرة
You will also have to pay a fine.	lāzem teddfa' ɣarāma kaman
	لازم تدفع غرامة كمان
Okay.	tamām
	تمام
Where are you going?	enta rāyeḥ feyn?
	إنت رايح فين؟
I'm going to …	ana rāyeḥ le...
	أنا رايح لـ...
How much? I don't understand.	bekām? ana meʃ fāhem
	بكام؟ أنا مش فاهم
Write it down, please.	ektebha laww samaḥt
	إكتبها لو سمحت
Okay. Can I pay with a credit card?	tamām. momken addfa' be kredit kard?
	تمام. ممكن أدفع بكريدت كارد؟
Yes, you can.	aywā momken
	أيوة ممكن
Here's your receipt.	ettfaddal el īsāl
	اتفضل الإيصال
Sorry about the fine.	'āssef bexeṣūṣ el ɣarāma
	آسف بخصوص الغرامة
That's okay. It was my fault.	mafīʃ moʃkela. di ɣalṭety
	ما فيش مشكلة. دي غلطتي
Enjoy your trip.	esstammte' be reḥlatek
	استمتع برحلتك

Taxi

taxi	taksi تاكسي
taxi driver	sawwā' el taksi سواق التاكسي
to catch a taxi	'āxod taksi أخد تاكسي
taxi stand	maw'af taksi موقف تاكسي
Where can I get a taxi?	meneyn āxod taksi? منين أخد تاكسي؟

to call a taxi	an tattlob taksi أن تطلب تاكسي
I need a taxi.	ahtāg taksi أحتاج تاكسي
Right now.	al'āan الآن
What is your address (location)?	ma howa 'ennwānak? ما هو عنوانك؟
My address is ...	'ennwāny fi ... عنواني في ...
Your destination?	ettegāhak? إتجاهك؟
Excuse me, ...	ba'd ezznak, ... بعد إذنك، ...
Are you available?	enta fādy? إنت فاضي؟
How much is it to get to ...?	bekām arūh...? بكام أروح...؟
Do you know where it is?	te'raf hiya feyn? تعرف هي فين؟

Airport, please.	el matār men fadlak المطار من فضلك
Stop here, please.	wa'eff hena, laww samaht وقف هنا، لو سمحت
It's not here.	mef hena مش هنا
This is the wrong address.	da 'enwān yalat دة عنوان غلط
Turn left.	oddxol femal ادخل شمال
Turn right.	oddxol yemīn ادخل يمين

How much do I owe you?	'layī līk ḳām? علىَّ لك كام؟
I'd like a receipt, please.	'āyez īṣāl men faḍlak. عايز إيصال، من فضلك.
Keep the change.	ḳally el bā'y خلّي الباقي

Would you please wait for me?	momken tesstannāny laww samaḥt? ممكن تستنّاني لو سمحت؟
five minutes	ḳamas daqā'eq خمس دقائق
ten minutes	'aʃar daqā'eq عشر دقائق
fifteen minutes	rob' sā'a ربع ساعة
twenty minutes	telt sā'a تلت ساعة
half an hour	noṣṣ sā'a نص ساعة

Hotel

Hello.	ahlan أهلا
My name is ...	essmy ... ... إسمي
I have a reservation.	'andy ḥaggz عندي حجز
I need ...	meḥtāg ... ... محتاج
a single room	ɣorfa moffrada غرفة مفردة
a double room	ɣorfa mozzdawwaga غرفة مزدوجة
How much is that?	se'raha kām? سعرها كام؟
That's a bit expensive.	di ɣalya ʃewaya دي غالية شوية
Do you have anything else?	'andak xayarāt tanya? عندك خيارات تانية؟
I'll take it.	haxod-ha ح أخدها
I'll pay in cash.	ḥaddfa' naqqdy ح أدفع نقدي
I've got a problem.	ana 'andy moʃkela أنا عندي مشكلة
My ... is broken.	... maksūr ...مكسور
My ... is out of order.	... 'aṭlān /'aṭlāna/ ...أطلان /عطلانة/
TV	el televizyōn التليفزيون
air conditioner	el takyīf التكييف
tap	el ḥanafiya (~ 'aṭlāna) الحنفية
shower	el doʃ الدش
sink	el banyo البانيو
safe	el xāzena (~ 'aṭlāna) الخازنة

door lock	'effl el bāb قفل الباب
electrical outlet	maxrag el kahraba مخرج الكهربا
hairdryer	mogaffef el ʃaʿr مجفف الشعر

I don't have …	maʿandīʃ … ما عنديش …
water	maya ميّة
light	nūr نور
electricity	kahraba كهربا

Can you give me …?	momken teddīny …? ممكن تديني …؟
a towel	fūṭa فوطة
a blanket	baṭṭaneya بطّانية
slippers	ʃebʃeb شبشب
a robe	robe روب
shampoo	ʃambū شامبو
soap	ṣabūn صابون

I'd like to change rooms.	aḥebb ayayar el oḍa أحب أغيّر الأوضة
I can't find my key.	meʃ lā'y meftāḥy مش لاقي مفتاحي
Could you open my room, please?	momken tefftaḥ oḍḍty men faḍlak? ممكن تفتح أوضتي من فضلك؟
Who's there?	meyn henāk? مين هناك؟
Come in!	ettfaḍḍal! إتفضل!
Just a minute!	daqīqa wāḥeda! دقيقة واحدة!
Not right now, please.	meʃ dellwa'ty men faḍlak مش دلوقتي من فضلك

Come to my room, please.	taʿāla oḍḍty laww samaḥt تعالى أوضتي لو سمحت
I'd like to order food service.	'āyez ṭalab men xeddmet el wagabāt عايز طلب من خدمة الوجبات
My room number is …	raqam oḍḍty howa … رقم أوضتي هو …

I'm leaving ...	ana māʃy ... **أنا ماشي ...**
We're leaving ...	eḥna maʃyīn ... **إحنا ماشيين ...**
right now	dellwa'ty **دلوقتي**
this afternoon	ba'd el ẓohr **بعد الظهر**
tonight	el leyla di **الليلة دي**
tomorrow	bokra **بكرة**
tomorrow morning	bokra el ṣobh **بكرة الصبح**
tomorrow evening	bokra bel leyl **بكرة بالليل**
the day after tomorrow	ba'd bokra **بعد بكرة**

I'd like to pay.	aḥebb adfa' **أحب أدفع**
Everything was wonderful.	kol ʃey' kan rā'e' **كل شيء كان رائع**
Where can I get a taxi?	feyn momken alā'y taksi? **فين ممكن ألاقي تاكسي؟**
Would you call a taxi for me, please?	momken toṭlob lī taksi laww samaḥt? **ممكن تطلب لي تاكسي لو سمحت؟**

Restaurant

Can I look at the menu, please?	momken aʃūf qāʼema el ṭaʻām men faḍlak? ممكن أشوف قائمة الطعام من فضلك؟
Table for one.	tarabeyza le ʃaxs wāḥed ترابيزة لشخص واحد
There are two (three, four) of us.	eḥnạ etneyn (talāta, arbaʻa) إحنا اتنين (ثلاثة، أربعة)

Smoking	modaxenīn مدخنين
No smoking	ɣeyr moddaxenīn غير مدخنين
Excuse me! (addressing a waiter)	laww samaḥt لو سمحت
menu	qāʼemat el ṭaʻām قائمة الطعام
wine list	qāʼemat el nebīz قائمة النبيذ
The menu, please.	el qāʼema, laww samaḥt القائمة، لو سمحت

Are you ready to order?	mosstaʻed toṭṭlob? مستعد تطلب؟
What will you have?	hataxod eh? ح تاخد إيه؟
I'll have ...	ana ḥaxod ... أنا ح آخد ...

I'm a vegetarian.	ana nạbāty أنا نباتي
meat	laḥma لحم
fish	samakk سمك
vegetables	xoḍār خضار
Do you have vegetarian dishes?	ʻandak aṭṭbāq nabātiya? عندك أطباق نباتية؟
I don't eat pork.	lā ʼāakol ẹl xanzīr لا أكل الخنزير
He /she/ doesn't eat meat.	howwa /hiya/ la tākol el laḥm هو/هي/ لا تأكل اللحم

I am allergic to ...	'andy ḥasasseya men ... عندي حساسية من ...
Would you please bring me ...	momken tegīb lī ... ممكن تجيب لي...
salt	pepper	sugar	melḥ	felfel	sokkar سكر ا فلفل ا ملح
coffee	tea	dessert	'ahwa	ʃāy	ḥelw حلو ا شاي ا قهوة
water	sparkling	plain	meyāh	ɣaziya	'adiya عادية ا غازية ا مياه
a spoon	fork	knife	maʻlaʻa	ʃowka	sekkīna سكينة ا شوكة ا ملعقة
a plate	napkin	ṭabaq	fūṭa فوطةا طبق

Enjoy your meal!	bel hana wel ʃefa بالهنا والشفا
One more, please.	waḥda kamān laww samaḥt واحدة كمان لو سمحت
It was very delicious.	kanet lazīza geddan كانت لذيذة جدا

check	change	tip	ʃīk	fakka	ba'ʃīʃ بقشيشا فكةا شيك
Check, please. (Could I have the check, please?)	momken el ḥesāb laww samaḥt? ممكن الحساب لو سمحت؟
Can I pay by credit card?	momken addfaʻ be kart e'temān? ممكن أدفع بكارت إئتمان؟
I'm sorry, there's a mistake here.	ana 'āssif, feyh ɣalṭa hena أنا آسف، في غلطة هنا

Shopping

Can I help you?	momken asa'dak?
	ممكن أساعدك؟
Do you have ...?	ya tara 'andak ...?
	يا ترى عندك ...؟
I'm looking for ...	ana badawwar 'la ...
	أنا بادور على ...
I need ...	mehtāg ...
	محتاج ...

I'm just looking.	ana battfarrag
	أنا بأتفرج
We're just looking.	ehna benettfarrag
	إحنا بنتفرج
I'll come back later.	hāgy ba'deyn
	ح أجي بعدين
We'll come back later.	haneygy ba'deyn
	ح نيجي بعدين
discounts | sale	taxfīdāt | okazyōn
	أوكازيونا تخفيضات

Would you please show me ...	momken tewarrīny ... laww samaht?
	ممكن توريني ... لو سمحت؟
Would you please give me ...	momken teddīny ... laww samaht
	ممكن تديني ... لو سمحت
Can I try it on?	momken a'īs?
	ممكن أقيس؟
Excuse me, where's the fitting room?	laww samaht, feyn el brova?
	لو سمحت، فين البروفا؟
Which color would you like?	'āyez ayī lone?
	عايز أي لون؟
size | length	maqās | tūl
	طول ا مقاس
How does it fit?	ya tara el maqās mazbūt?
	يا ترى المقاس مضبوط؟

How much is it?	bekām?
	بكام؟
That's too expensive.	da ɣāly geddan
	دة غالي جدا
I'll take it.	haftereyh
	ح أشتريه
Excuse me, where do I pay?	ba'd ezznak, addfa' feyn laww samaht?
	بعد إذنك، أدفع فين لو سمحت؟

Will you pay in cash or credit card?	hateddfa' naqqdan walla be kart e'temān? ح تدفع نقدا ولا بكارت إئتمان؟
In cash | with credit card	naqdan | be kart e'temān بكارت إئتمان | نقدا

Do you want the receipt?	'āyez īṣāl? عايز إيصال؟
Yes, please.	aywā, men faḍlak أيوة، من فضلك
No, it's OK.	lā, mafīʃ moʃkela لا، ما فيش مشكلة
Thank you. Have a nice day!	ʃokran. yome sa'īd شكرا. يوم سعيد

In town

Excuse me, please.	ba'd ezznak, laww samaḥt بعد إذنك، لو سمحت
I'm looking for ...	ana badawwar 'la ... أنا بادور على ...

the subway	metro el anfā' مترو الأنفاق
my hotel	el fondo' betā'i الفندق بتاعي
the movie theater	el sinema السينما
a taxi stand	maw'af taksi موقف تاكسي

an ATM	makīnet ṣarraf 'āaly ماكينة صراف آلي
a foreign exchange office	maktab ṣarrafa مكتب صرافة
an internet café	maqha internet مقهى انترنت
... street	ʃāre'... ... شارع
this place	el makān da المكان دة

Do you know where ... is?	hal te'raf feyn ...? هل تعرف فين ...؟
Which street is this?	essmu eyh el ʃāre' da? اسمه إيه الشارع دة؟

Show me where we are right now.	momken tewarrīny eḥna feyn dellwa'ty? ممكن توريني إحنا فين دلوقتي؟
Can I get there on foot?	momken awṣal ḥenāk māʃy? ممكن أوصل هناك ماشي؟
Do you have a map of the city?	'andak xarīṭa lel madīna? عندك خريطة للمدينة؟

How much is a ticket to get in?	bekām tazkaret el doxūl? بكام تذكرة الدخول؟
Can I take pictures here?	momken aṣṣawwar hena? ممكن أصور هنا؟
Are you open?	entom fatt-ḥīn? إنتم فاتحين؟

When do you open?

emta betefftaḥu?
إمتى بتفتحوا؟

When do you close?

emta bete'ffelu?
إمتى بتقفلوا؟

Money

money	folūss فلوس
cash	naqdy نقدي
paper money	folūss waraqiya فلوس ورقية
loose change	fakka فكة
check | change | tip	ʃik | fakka | ba'ʃiʃ بقشيش|ا فكة|ا شيك
credit card	kart e'temān كارت إئتمان
wallet	maḥfaza محفظة
to buy	ʃerā' شراء
to pay	daf' دفع
fine	ɣarāma غرامة
free	maggānan مجانا
Where can I buy ...?	feyn momken aʃtery ...? فين ممكن أشتري ...؟
Is the bank open now?	hal el bank fāteḥ dellwa'ty هل البنك فاتح دلوقتي؟
When does it open?	emta betefftaḥ? إمتى بيفتح؟
When does it close?	emta beye'ffel? إمتى بيقفل؟
How much?	bekām? بكام؟
How much is this?	bekām da? بكام دة؟
That's too expensive.	da ɣāly geddan دة غالي جدا
Excuse me, where do I pay?	ba'd ezznak, addfa' feyn laww samaḥt? بعد إذنك، أدفع فين لو سمحت؟
Check, please.	el ḥesāb men faḍlak الحساب من فضلك

Can I pay by credit card?	momken addfa' be kart e'temān? ممكن أدفع بكارت إئتمان؟
Is there an ATM here?	feyh hena makīnet ṣarraf 'āaly? فيه هنا ماكينة صراف آلي؟
I'm looking for an ATM.	baddawwar 'la makīnet ṣarraf 'ālly بادور على ماكينة صراف آلي

I'm looking for a foreign exchange office.	baddawwar 'la maktab ṣarrāfa بادور على مكتب صرافة
I'd like to change ...	'āyez aɣayar ... عايز أغير ...
What is the exchange rate?	se'r el 'omla kām? سعر العملة كام؟
Do you need my passport?	enta mehtāg gawāz safary? إنت محتاج جواز سفري؟

Time

What time is it?	el sā'a kām? الساعة كام؟
When?	emta? إمتى؟
At what time?	fi ayī sā'a? في أي ساعة؟
now | later | after ...	dellwa'ty | ba'deyn | ba'd ... ... بعد ا بعدين ا دلوقتي

one o'clock	el sā'a waḥda الساعة واحدة
one fifteen	el sā'a waḥda we rob' الساعة واحدة وربع
one thirty	el sā'a waḥda we noṣṣ الساعة واحدة ونص
one forty-five	el sā'a etneyn ellā rob' الساعة إتنين إلا ربع

one | two | three	waḥda | etneyn | talāta تلاتة اتنين ا واحدة
four | five | six	arba'a | χamsa | setta ستة اخمسة الأربعة
seven | eight | nine	sabb'a | tamanya | tess'a تسعة تمانية ا سبعة
ten | eleven | twelve	'aʃra | hedāʃar | etnāʃar اتناشر ا حداشر ا عشرة

in ...	fi ... في ...
five minutes	χamas daqā'eq خمس دقائق
ten minutes	'aʃar daqā'eq عشر دقائق
fifteen minutes	rob' sā'a ربع ساعة
twenty minutes	telt sā'a تلت ساعة

half an hour	noṣṣ sā'a نص ساعة
an hour	sā'a ساعة

in the morning	el sobh
	الصبح
early in the morning	el sobh badri
	الصبح بدري
this morning	el naharda el sobh
	النهاردة الصبح
tomorrow morning	bokra el sobh
	بكرة الصبح

in the middle of the day	fi noss el yome
	في نص اليوم
in the afternoon	ba'd el zohr
	بعد الظهر
in the evening	bel leyl
	بالليل
tonight	el leyla di
	الليلة دي

at night	bel leyl
	بالليل
yesterday	emmbāreh
	إمبارح
today	el naharda
	النهاردة
tomorrow	bokra
	بكرة
the day after tomorrow	ba'd bokra
	بعد بكرة

What day is it today?	el naharda eyh fel ayām?
	النهاردة إيه في الأيام؟
It's ...	el naharda ...
	النهاردة ...
Monday	el etneyn
	الإتنين
Tuesday	el talāt
	التلات
Wednesday	el 'arba'
	الأربع

Thursday	el xamīs
	الخميس
Friday	el gumu'ā
	الجمعة
Saturday	el sabt
	السبت
Sunday	el hadd
	الحد

Greetings. Introductions

Hello.	ahlan أهلا
Pleased to meet you.	sa'īd be leqā'ak سعيد بلقائك
Me too.	ana ass'ad أنا أسعد
I'd like you to meet ...	a'arrafak be ... أعرفك بـ ...
Nice to meet you.	forṣa sa'īda فرصة سعيدة
How are you?	ezzayak? إزيك؟
My name is ...	esmy ... أسمي ...
His name is ...	essmu ... إسمه ...
Her name is ...	essmaha ... إسمها ...
What's your name?	essmak eyh? إسمك إيه؟
What's his name?	essmu eyh? إسمه إيه؟
What's her name?	essmaha eyh? إسمها إيه؟
What's your last name?	essm 'ā'eltak eyh? إسم عائلتك إيه؟
You can call me ...	te'ddar tenadīny be... تقدر تناديني بـ....
Where are you from?	enta meneyn? إنت منين؟
I'm from ...	ana men ... أنا من ...
What do you do for a living?	beteʃtayal eh? بتشتغل إيه؟
Who is this?	meyn da مين دة
Who is he?	meyn howwa? مين هو؟
Who is she?	meyn hiya? مين هي؟
Who are they?	meyn homm? مين هم؟

This is ...	da yeb'ā ... دة يبقى ...
my friend (masc.)	ṣadīqy صديقي
my friend (fem.)	ṣadīqaty صديقتي
my husband	gouzy جوزي
my wife	merāty مراتي

my father	waldy والدي
my mother	waldety والدتي
my brother	axūya أخويا
my son	ebny إبني
my daughter	bennty بنتي

This is our son.	da ebnena دة إبننا
This is our daughter.	di benntena دي بنتتنا
These are my children.	dole awwlādy دول أولادي
These are our children.	dole awwladna دول أولادنا

Farewells

Good bye!	ella alliqā' إلى اللقاء
Bye! (inform.)	salām سلام
See you tomorrow.	aʃūfak bokra أشوفك بكرة
See you soon.	aʃūfak orayeb أشوفك قريب
See you at seven.	aʃūfak el sā'a sab'a أشوفك الساعة سبعة
Have fun!	esstammte'! إستمتع!
Talk to you later.	netkallem ba'deyn نتكلم بعدين
Have a nice weekend.	'ottlet osbū' sa'īda عطلة أسبوع سعيدة
Good night.	tessbah 'la xeyr تصبح على خير
It's time for me to go.	gā' waqt el zehāb جاء وقت الذهاب
I have to go.	lāzem amʃy لازم أمشي
I will be right back.	harga' 'la tūl ح أرجع على طول
It's late.	el waqt mett'axar الوقت متأخر
I have to get up early.	lāzem ass-ha badry لازم أصحى بدري
I'm leaving tomorrow.	ana māʃy bokra أنا ماشي بكرة
We're leaving tomorrow.	ehhna maʃyīn bokra إحنا ماشيين بكرة
Have a nice trip!	rehla sa'īda! إرحلة سعيدة
It was nice meeting you.	forsa sa'īda فرصة سعيدة
It was nice talking to you.	sa'eddt bel kalām ma'ak سعدت بالكلام معك
Thanks for everything.	ʃokran 'la koll ʃey' شكرا على كل شيء

I had a very good time.	ana qaḍḍayt waqt saʿīd
	أنا قضيت وقت سعيد
We had a very good time.	ehna 'aḍḍeyna wa't saʿīd
	إحنا قضينا وقت سعيد
It was really great.	kan bel feʿl rāʾeʿ
	كان بالفعل رائع
I'm going to miss you.	hatewwhaʃīny
	ح توحشني
We're going to miss you.	hatewwhaʃna
	ح توحشنا

Good luck!	ḥazz saʿīd!
	حظ سعيد!
Say hi to ...	taḥīāty le...
	تحياتي لـ...

Foreign language

I don't understand.	ana meʃ fāhem أنا مش فاهم
Write it down, please.	ektebha laww samaḥt إكتبها لو سمحت
Do you speak …?	enta betettkalem …? انت بتتكلم …؟

I speak a little bit of …	ana battkallem ʃewaya … أنا باتكلم شوية …
English	engilīzy أنجليزي
Turkish	torky تركي
Arabic	ʿaraby عربي
French	faransāwy فرنساوي

German	almāny ألماني
Italian	iṭāly إيطالي
Spanish	asbāny أسباني
Portuguese	bortoɣāly برتغالي
Chinese	ṣīny صيني
Japanese	yabāny ياباني

Can you repeat that, please.	momken teʿīd el kalām men faḍlak? ممكن تعيد الكلام من فضلك؟
I understand.	ana fāhem انا فاهم
I don't understand.	ana meʃ fāhem انا مش فاهم
Please speak more slowly.	momken tetkallem abṭa' laww samaḥt? ممكن تتكلم ابطأ لو سمحت؟

Is that correct? (Am I saying it right?)	keda ṣaḥḥ? كدة صح؟
What is this? (What does this mean?)	eh da? إيه دة؟

Apologies

Excuse me, please.	ba'd ezznak, laww samaḥt بعد إذنك، لو سمحت
I'm sorry.	ana 'āṣṣif أنا آسف
I'm really sorry.	ana 'āṣṣif beggad أنا آسف بجد
Sorry, it's my fault.	ana 'āṣṣif, di ɣalṭeti أنا آسف، دي غلطتي
My mistake.	ɣalṭety غلطتي
May I ...?	momken ...? ممكن ...؟
Do you mind if I ...?	teḍḍāyi' laww ...? تتضايق لو ...؟
It's OK.	mafīʃ moʃkela ما فيش مشكلة
It's all right.	kollo tamām كله تمام
Don't worry about it.	mate'la'ʃ ما تقلقش

Agreement

Yes.	aywā أيوة
Yes, sure.	aywa, akīd ايوة، أكيد
OK (Good!)	tamām تمام
Very well.	kowayīs geddan كويس جدا
Certainly!	bekol ta'kīd! إبكل تأكيد!
I agree.	mewāfe' موافق

That's correct.	da ṣaḥīḥ دة صحيح
That's right.	da ṣaḥḥ دة صح
You're right.	kalāmak ṣaḥḥ كلامك صح
I don't mind.	ma'andīʃ māne' ما عنديش مانع
Absolutely right.	ṣaḥḥ tamāman صح تماماً

It's possible.	momken ممكن
That's a good idea.	di fekra kewayīsa دي فكرة كويسة
I can't say no.	ma'darʃ a'ūl la' ما أقدرش أقول لأ
I'd be happy to.	bekol sorūr حكون سعيد
With pleasure.	bekol sorūr بكل سرور

Refusal. Expressing doubt

No.	la'a لا
Certainly not.	akīd la' أكيد لأ
I don't agree.	meʃ mewāfe' مش موافق
I don't think so.	ma 'azzonneʃ keda ما أظنش كدة
It's not true.	da meʃ ṣaḥīḥ دة مش صحيح
You are wrong.	enta ɣalṭān إنت غلطان
I think you are wrong.	azonn ennak ɣalṭān أظن إنك غلطان
I'm not sure.	meʃ akīd مش أكيد
It's impossible.	da mos-taḥīl دة مستحيل
Nothing of the kind (sort)!	mafīʃ ḥāga keda! ما فيش حاجة كدة!
The exact opposite.	el 'akss tamāman العكس تماما
I'm against it.	ana dedd da أنا ضد دة
I don't care.	ma yehemmenīʃ ما يهمنيش
I have no idea.	ma'andīʃ fekra ما عنديش فكرة
I doubt it.	aʃokk fe da أشك في دة
Sorry, I can't.	'āssef ma 'qdarʃ آسف، ما أقدرش
Sorry, I don't want to.	'āssef meʃ 'ayez آسف، مش عايز
Thank you, but I don't need this.	ʃokran, bass ana meʃ meḥtāg loh شكرا، بس أنا مش محتاج له
It's getting late.	el waqt mett'aχar الوقت متأخر

I have to get up early.

lāzem aṣṣ-ha badry

لازم أصحى بدري

I don't feel well.

ana ta'bān

أنا تعبان

Expressing gratitude

Thank you.	ʃokran شكراً
Thank you very much.	ʃokran gazīlan شكراً جزيلاً
I really appreciate it.	ana ha'i'i me'addar da أنا حقيقي مقدر دة
I'm really grateful to you.	ana mommtann līk geddan أنا ممتن لك جداً
We are really grateful to you.	ehna mommtannīn līk geddan إحنا ممتنين لك جداً
Thank you for your time.	ʃokran 'la wa'tak شكراً على وقتك
Thanks for everything.	ʃokran 'la koll ʃey' شكراً على كل شيء
Thank you for ...	ʃokran 'la ... شكراً على ...
your help	mosa'detak مساعدتك
a nice time	el waqt الوقت اللطيف
a wonderful meal	wagba rā'e'a وجبة رائعة
a pleasant evening	amsiya mummte'a أمسية ممتعة
a wonderful day	yome rā'e' يوم رائع
an amazing journey	rehla mod-heʃa رحلة مدهشة
Don't mention it.	lā ʃokr 'la wāgeb لا شكر على واجب
You are welcome.	el 'afw العفو
Any time.	ayī waqt أي وقت
My pleasure.	bekol sorūr بكل سرور
Forget it.	ennsa إنسى
Don't worry about it.	mate'la'ʃ ما تقلقش

Congratulations. Best wishes

Congratulations!	ohannīk! أهنيك!
Happy birthday!	ʿīd milād saʿīd! عيد ميلاد سعيد!
Merry Christmas!	ʿīd milād saʿīd! عيد ميلاد سعيد!
Happy New Year!	sana gedīda saʿīda! سنة جديدة سعيدة!
Happy Easter!	ʃamm nessīm saʿīd! شم نسيم سعيد!
Happy Hanukkah!	hanūka saʿīda! هانوكا سعيدة!
I'd like to propose a toast.	aḥebb aqtareḥ neʃrab naxab أحب أقترح نشرب نخب
Cheers!	fi seḥḥettak في صحتك
Let's drink to ...!	yalla neʃrab fe ...! ياللا نشرب في ...!
To our success!	nagāḥna نجاحنا
To your success!	nagāḥak نجاحك
Good luck!	ḥazz saʿīd! حظ سعيد!
Have a nice day!	nahārak saʿīd! نهارك سعيد!
Have a good holiday!	agāza ṭayeba! أجازة طيبة!
Have a safe journey!	trūḥ bel salāma! تروح بالسلامة!
I hope you get better soon!	atmanna ennak taṭaʿāfa besorʿa! أتمنى إنك تتعافى بسرعة!

Socializing

Why are you sad?
enta leyh za'lān?
إنت ليه زعلان؟

Smile! Cheer up!
ebbtassem! farrfeʃ!
إبتسم! فرفش!

Are you free tonight?
enta fādy el leyla di?
إنت فاضي الليلة دي؟

May I offer you a drink?
momken a'zemak 'la maʃrūb?
ممكن أعزمك على مشروب؟

Would you like to dance?
tehebb torr'oss?
تحب ترقص؟

Let's go to the movies.
yalla nerūh el sinema
ياللا نروح السينما

May I invite you to ...?
momken a'zemak 'la ...?
ممكن أعزمك على ...؟

a restaurant
mattʻam
مطعم

the movies
el sinema
السينما

the theater
el masrah
المسرح

go for a walk
tamʃeya
تمشية

At what time?
fi ayī sā'a?
في أي ساعة؟

tonight
el leyla di
الليلة دي

at six
el sā'a setta
الساعة ستة

at seven
el sā'a sab'a
الساعة سبعة

at eight
el sā'a tamanya
الساعة تمانية

at nine
el sā'a tess'a
الساعة تسعة

Do you like it here?
ya tara 'agbak el makān?
يا ترى عاجبك المكان؟

Are you here with someone?
enta hena ma' hadd?
إنت هنا مع حد؟

I'm with my friend.
ana ma' sadīq
أنا مع صديق

I'm with my friends.	ana ma' aşşdiqā' أنا مع أصدقاء
No, I'm alone.	lā, ana waḥḥdy لا، أنا وحدي
Do you have a boyfriend?	hal 'andak şadīq? هل عندك صديق؟
I have a boyfriend.	ana 'andy şadīq أنا عندي صديق
Do you have a girlfriend?	hal 'andak şadīqa? هل عندك صديقة؟
I have a girlfriend.	ana 'andy şadīqa أنا عندي صديقة
Can I see you again?	a'dar aʃūfak tāny? أقدر أشوفك تاني؟
Can I call you?	a'dar atteşel bīk? أقدر أتصل بك؟
Call me. (Give me a call.)	ettaşşel bī إتصل بي
What's your number?	eh raqamek? إيه رقمك؟
I miss you.	waḥaʃtīny وحشتني
You have a beautiful name.	essmek gamīl إسمك جميل
I love you.	oheḅbek أحبك
Will you marry me?	tettgawwezīny? تتجوزيني؟
You're kidding!	enta bett-hazzar! إنت بتهزر!
I'm just kidding.	ana bahazzar bas أنا باهزر بس
Are you serious?	enta bettettkallem gad? إنت بتتكلم جد؟
I'm serious.	ana gād أنا جاد
Really?!	şahīḥ? صحيح؟
It's unbelievable!	meʃ ma''ūl! مش معقول!
I don't believe you.	ana meʃ meşşad'āk أنا مش مصدقاك
I can't.	ma'darʃ ما أقدرش
I don't know.	ma'rafʃ ما أعرفش
I don't understand you.	meʃ fahmāk مش فاهماك

Please go away.

men faḍlak temʃy

من فضلك تمشي

Leave me alone!

sebbny lewaḥḥdy!

!سيبني لوحدي

I can't stand him.

ana lā aṭīqo

أنا لا أطيقه

You are disgusting!

enta mo'reff

إنت مقرف

I'll call the police!

haṭṭlob el ʃorta

ح أطلب الشرطة

Sharing impressions. Emotions

I like it.	ye'gebny يعجبني
Very nice.	laṭīf geddan لطيف جدا
That's great!	da rā'e' دة رائع
It's not bad.	da meʃ saye' دة مش سيء
I don't like it.	meʃ 'agebny مش عاجبني
It's not good.	meʃ kowayīs مش كويس
It's bad.	da saye' دة سيء
It's very bad.	da saye' geddan دة سيء جدا
It's disgusting.	da mo'rreff دة مقرف
I'm happy.	ana saʿīd أنا سعيد
I'm content.	ana mabsūṭ أنا مبسوط
I'm in love.	ana baḥebb أنا باحب
I'm calm.	ana hādy أنا هادي
I'm bored.	ana zah'ān أنا زهقان
I'm tired.	ana ta'bān أنا تعبان
I'm sad.	ana ḥazīn أنا حزين
I'm frightened.	ana χāyef أنا خايف
I'm angry.	ana ɣadbān أنا غضبان
I'm worried.	ana qalqān أنا قلقان
I'm nervous.	ana muṭawwatter أنا متوتر

I'm jealous. (envious)

ana γayrān
أنا غيران

I'm surprised.

ana mutafāge'
أنا متفاجئ

I'm perplexed.

ana morrtabek
أنا مرتبك

Problems. Accidents

I've got a problem.	ana 'andy moʃkela أنا عندي مشكلة
We've got a problem.	ehna 'andena moʃkela إحنا عندنا مشكلة
I'm lost.	ana tāʒeh أنا تايه
I missed the last bus (train).	fātny 'āaxer otobiis فاتني آخر أوتوبيس
I don't have any money left.	meʃ fāḍel ma'aya flūss مش فاضل معايا فلوس

I've lost my ...	ḍā' menny ... betā'y ضاع مني ... بتاعي
Someone stole my ...	ḥadd sara' ... betā'y حد سرق ... بتاعي
passport	bassbore باسبور
wallet	maḥfaza محفظة
papers	awwarā' أوراق
ticket	tazzkara تذكرة

money	folūss فلوس
handbag	ʃannṭa شنطة
camera	kamera كاميرا
laptop	lab tob لاب توب
tablet computer	tablet تابلت
mobile phone	telefon maḥmūl تليفون محمول

Help me!	sā'dny! ساعدني!
What's happened?	eh elly ḥaṣal? إيه إللي حصل؟
fire	harīqa حريقة

shooting	ḍarrb nār
	ضرب نار
murder	qattl
	قتل
explosion	ennfegār
	إنفجار
fight	xenā'a
	خناقة

Call the police!	ettaṣel bel ʃorṭa!
	!اتصل بالشرطة
Please hurry up!	besor'a men faḍlak!
	!بسرعة من فضلك
I'm looking for the police station.	baddawwar 'la qessm el ʃorṭa
	بادور على قسم الشرطة
I need to make a call.	mehtāg a'mel mokalma telefoneya
	محتاج أعمل مكالمة تليفونية
May I use your phone?	momken asstaxdem telefonak?
	ممكن أستخدم تليفونك؟

I've been ...	ana kont ...
	أنا كنت ...
mugged	ettnaʃalt
	اتنشلت
robbed	ettsaraqt
	اتسرقت
raped	oxtiṣabt
	اغتصبت
attacked (beaten up)	ta'arraḍt le e'tedā'
	تعرضت لإعتداء

Are you all right?	enta bexeyr?
	إنت بخير؟
Did you see who it was?	ya tara ʃoft meyn?
	يا ترى شفت مين؟
Would you be able to recognize the person?	te'ddar tett'arraf 'la el ʃaxṣ da?
	تقدر تتعرف على الشخص دة؟
Are you sure?	enta muta'kked?
	إنت متأكد؟

Please calm down.	argūk ehḍa
	أرجوك إهدا
Take it easy!	hawwen 'aleyk!
	!اهون عليك
Don't worry!	mate'la'ʃ!
	!ما تقلقش
Everything will be fine.	kol ʃey' haykūn tamām
	كل شيء ح يكون تمام
Everything's all right.	kol ʃey' tamām
	كل شيء تمام
Come here, please.	ta'āla hena laww samaḥt
	تعالى هنا لو سمحت

I have some questions for you.

'andy līk as'ela

عندي لك أسئلة

Wait a moment, please.

esstanna laḥza men faḍlak

إستنى لحظة من فضلك

Do you have any I.D.?

'andak raqam qawwmy

عندك رقم قومي

Thanks. You can leave now.

ʃokran. momken temʃy dellwa'ty

شكرا. ممكن تمشي دلوقتي

Hands behind your head!

eydeyk wara rāsak!

إيديك ورا راسك

You're under arrest!

enta maqbūḍ 'aleyk!

إنت مقبوض عليك

Health problems

Please help me.	argūk sā'dny أرجوك ساعدني
I don't feel well.	ana ta'bān أنا تعبان
My husband doesn't feel well.	gouzy ta'bān جوزي تعبان
My son ...	ebny ... إبني ...
My father ...	waldy ... والدي ...

My wife doesn't feel well.	merāty ta'bāna مراتي تعابة
My daughter ...	bennty ... بنتي ...
My mother ...	waldety ... والدتي ...

I've got a ...	ana 'andy ... أنا عندي ...
headache	ṣodā' صداع
sore throat	eḥtiqān fel zore إحتقان في الزور
stomach ache	mayaṣṣ مغص
toothache	alam asnān ألم أسنان

I feel dizzy.	ʃā'er be dawār شاعر بدوار
He has a fever.	'andak ḥomma عنده حمي
She has a fever.	'andaha ḥomma عندها حمي
I can't breathe.	meʃ 'āder attnaffess مش قادر أتنفس

I'm short of breath.	meʃ 'āder attnaffess مش قادر أتنفس
I am asthmatic.	ana 'andy azzma أنا عندي أزمة
I am diabetic.	ana 'andy el sokkar أنا عندي السكر

I can't sleep.	meʃ 'āder anām
	مش قادر أنام
food poisoning	tassammom yezā'y
	تسمم غذائي

It hurts here.	betewwga' hena
	بتوجع هنا
Help me!	sā'edny!
	!ساعدني
I am here!	ana ḥena!
	!أنا هنا
We are here!	eḥna hena!
	!إحنا هنا
Get me out of here!	xarragūny men hena
	خرجوني من هنا
I need a doctor.	ana meḥtāg ṭabīb
	أنا محتاج طبيب
I can't move.	meʃ 'āder at-ḥarrak
	مش قادر أتحرك
I can't move my legs.	meʃ 'āder aḥarrak reglaya
	مش قادر أحرك رجلية

I have a wound.	'andy garrḥḥ
	عندي جرح
Is it serious?	da beggad?
	دة بجد؟
My documents are in my pocket.	awwrā'y fi geyby
	أوراقي في جيبي
Calm down!	ehhda'!
	!إهدا
May I use your phone?	momken asstaxdem telefonak?
	ممكن أستخدم تليفونك؟

Call an ambulance!	oṭlob 'arabeyet es'āf!
	!أطلب عربية إسعاف
It's urgent!	di ḥāla messta'gela!
	!دي حالة مستعجلة
It's an emergency!	di ḥāla ṭāre'a!
	!دي حالة طارئة
Please hurry up!	besor'a men faḍlak!
	!إبسرعة من فضلك
Would you please call a doctor?	momken tekallem doktore men faḍlak?
	ممكن تكلم دكتور من فضلك؟
Where is the hospital?	feyn el mostaʃfa?
	فين المستشفى؟

How are you feeling?	ḥāsses be eyh dellwa'ty
	حاسس بإيه دلوقتي؟
Are you all right?	enta bexeyr?
	إنت بخير؟
What's happened?	eh elly ḥaṣal?
	إيه إللي حصل؟

I feel better now.

ana ḥāsseṣ eny aḥssan dellwa'ty

أنا حاسس إني أحسن دلوقتي

It's OK.

tamām

تمام

It's all right.

kollo tamām

كله تمام

At the pharmacy

pharmacy (drugstore)	ṣaydaliya صيدلية
24-hour pharmacy	ṣaydaliya arb'a we 'eʃrīn sā'a صيدلية 24 ساعة
Where is the closest pharmacy?	feyn aqrab ṣaydaliya? فين أقرب صيدلية؟
Is it open now?	hiya fat-ḥa dellwa'ty? هي فاتحة دلوقتي؟
At what time does it open?	betefftaḥ emta? بتفتح إمتى؟
At what time does it close?	bete'ffel emta? بتقفل إمتى؟
Is it far?	hiya be'eyda? هي بعيدة؟
Can I get there on foot?	momken awṣal henāk māʃy? ممكن أوصل هناك ماشي؟
Can you show me on the map?	momken tewarrīny 'lal xarīṭa? ممكن توريني على الخريطة؟
Please give me something for ...	men faḍlak eddīny ḥāga le... من فضلك إديني حاجة لـ...
a headache	el sodā' الصداع
a cough	el kohḥa الكحة
a cold	el bard البرد
the flu	influenza الأنفلوانزا
a fever	el ḥumma الحمى
a stomach ache	el mayaṣṣ المغص
nausea	el yasayān الغثيان
diarrhea	el es-hāl الإسهال
constipation	el emsāk الإمساك
pain in the back	alam fel zạhr ألم في الظهر

chest pain	alam fel ṣadr
	ألم في الصدر
side stitch	γorrza ganebiya
	غرزة جانبية
abdominal pain	alam fel baṭṭn
	ألم في البطن

pill	ḥabba
	حبة
ointment, cream	marham, krīm
	مرهم، كريم
syrup	ʃarāb
	شراب
spray	baχāχ
	بخاخ
drops	noqaṭṭ
	نقط

You need to go to the hospital.	enta mehtāg terūḥ
	انت محتاج تروح المستشفى
health insurance	ta'mīn ṣeḥhy
	تأمين صحي
prescription	roʃetta
	روشتة
insect repellant	ṭāred lel ḥaʃarāt
	طارد للحشرات
Band Aid	blastar
	بلاستر

The bare minimum

Excuse me, ...	ba'd ezznak, ... بعد إذنك، ...
Hello.	ahlan أهلا
Thank you.	ʃokran شكراً
Good bye.	ella alliqā' إلى اللقاء
Yes.	aywā أيوة
No.	la'a لا
I don't know.	ma'raʃʃ ما أعرفش
Where? | Where to? | When?	feyn? | lefeyn? | emta? إمتى؟ | لفين؟ | فين؟
I need ...	mehtāg ... محتاج ...
I want ...	'āyez ... عايز ...
Do you have ...?	ya tara 'andak ...? يا ترى عندك... ؟
Is there a ... here?	feyh hena ...? فيه هنا ...؟
May I ...?	momken ...? ممكن ...؟
..., please (polite request)	... men faḍlak من فضلك ...
I'm looking for ...	ana badawwar 'la ... أنا بادور على ...
restroom	hammām حمام
ATM	makīnet ṣarraf 'āaly ماكينة صراف آلي
pharmacy (drugstore)	ṣaydaliya صيدلية
hospital	mostaʃfa مستشفى
police station	'essm el ʃorṭa قسم شرطة
subway	metro el anfā' مترو الأنفاق

| taxi | taksi
تاكسي |
| train station | mahattet el 'attr
محطة القطر |

My name is ...	essmy ... إسمي...
What's your name?	essmak eyh? اسمك إيه؟
Could you please help me?	te'ddar tesā'dny? تقدر تساعدني؟
I've got a problem.	ana 'andy moʃkela أنا عندي مشكلة
I don't feel well.	ana ta'bān أنا تعبان
Call an ambulance!	otlob 'arabeyet es'āf! أطلب عربية إسعاف!
May I make a call?	momken a'mel mokalma telefoniya? ممكن أعمل مكالمة تليفونية؟

| I'm sorry. | ana 'āssif
أنا آسف |
| You're welcome. | el 'afw
العفو |

I, me	ana أنا
you (inform.)	enta أنت
he	howwa هو
she	hiya هي
they (masc.)	homm هم
they (fem.)	homm هم
we	ehna احنا
you (pl)	entom انتم
you (sg, form.)	haddretak حضرتك

ENTRANCE	doxūl دخول
EXIT	xorūg خروج
OUT OF ORDER	'attlān عطلان
CLOSED	moylaq مغلق

OPEN	maftūḥ
	مفتوح
FOR WOMEN	lel sayedāt
	للسيدات
FOR MEN	lel regāl
	للرجال

CONCISE
DICTIONARY

This section contains more
than 1,500 useful words
arranged alphabetically.
The dictionary includes a lot
of gastronomic terms and
will be helpful when ordering
food at a restaurant or buying
groceries

T&P Books Publishing

DICTIONARY CONTENTS

T&P Books Publishing

T&P Books Publishing

time	waqt (m)	وقت
hour	sā'a (f)	ساعة
half an hour	niṣf sā'a (m)	نصف ساعة
minute	daqīqa (f)	دقيقة
second	θāniya (f)	ثانية
today (adv)	al yawm	اليوم
tomorrow (adv)	ɣadan	غدًا
yesterday (adv)	ams	أمس
Monday	yawm al iθnayn (m)	يوم الإثنين
Tuesday	yawm aθ θulāθā' (m)	يوم الثلاثاء
Wednesday	yawm al arbi'ā' (m)	يوم الأربعاء
Thursday	yawm al χamīs (m)	يوم الخميس
Friday	yawm al ʒum'a (m)	يوم الجمعة
Saturday	yawm as sabt (m)	يوم السبت
Sunday	yawm al aḥad (m)	يوم الأحد
day	yawm (m)	يوم
working day	yawm 'amal (m)	يوم عمل
public holiday	yawm al 'uṭla ar rasmiyya (m)	يوم العطلة الرسمية
weekend	ayyām al 'uṭla (pl)	أيام العطلة
week	usbū' (m)	أسبوع
last week (adv)	fil isbū' al māḍi	في الأسبوع الماضي
next week (adv)	fil isbū' al qādim	في الأسبوع القادم
sunrise	ʃurūq aʃ ʃams (m)	شروق الشمس
sunset	ɣurūb aʃ ʃams (m)	غروب الشمس
in the morning	fiṣ ṣabāḥ	في الصباح
in the afternoon	ba'd aẓ ẓuhr	بعد الظهر
in the evening	fil masā'	في المساء
tonight (this evening)	al yawm fil masā'	اليوم في المساء
at night	bil layl	بالليل
midnight	muntaṣif al layl (m)	منتصف الليل
January	yanāyir (m)	يناير
February	fibrāyir (m)	فبراير
March	māris (m)	مارس
April	abrīl (m)	أبريل
May	māyu (m)	مايو

June	yūnyu (m)	يونيو
July	yūlyu (m)	يوليو
August	ayustus (m)	أغسطس
September	sibtambar (m)	سبتمبر
October	uktūbir (m)	أكتوبر
November	nuvimbar (m)	نوفمبر
December	disimbar (m)	ديسمبر
in spring	fir rabī'	في الربيع
in summer	fiṣ ṣayf	في الصيف
in fall	fil xarīf	في الخريف
in winter	fiʃ ʃitā'	في الشتاء
month	ʃahr (m)	شهر
season (summer, etc.)	faṣl (m)	فصل
year	sana (f)	سنة
century	qarn (m)	قرن

2. Numbers. Numerals

digit, figure	raqm (m)	رقم
number	'adad (m)	عدد
minus sign	nāqiṣ (m)	ناقص
plus sign	zā'id (m)	زائد
sum, total	maʒmū' (m)	مجموع
first (adj)	awwal	أوّل
second (adj)	θāni	ثان
third (adj)	θāliθ	ثالث
0 zero	ṣifr	صفر
1 one	wāḥid	واحد
2 two	iθnān	إثنان
3 three	θalāθa	ثلاثة
4 four	arba'a	أربعة
5 five	xamsa	خمسة
6 six	sitta	ستّة
7 seven	sab'a	سبعة
8 eight	θamāniya	ثمانية
9 nine	tis'a	تسعة
10 ten	'aʃara	عشرة
11 eleven	aḥad 'aʃar	أحد عشر
12 twelve	iθnā 'aʃar	إثنا عشر
13 thirteen	θalāθat 'aʃar	ثلاثة عشر
14 fourteen	arba'at 'aʃar	أربعة عشر
15 fifteen	xamsat 'aʃar	خمسة عشر
16 sixteen	sittat 'aʃar	ستّة عشر
17 seventeen	sab'at 'aʃar	سبعة عشر

| 18 eighteen | θamāniyat 'aʃar | ثمانية عشر |
| 19 nineteen | tis'at 'aʃar | تسعة عشر |

20 twenty	'iʃrūn	عشرون
30 thirty	θalāθīn	ثلاثون
40 forty	arba'ūn	أربعون
50 fifty	χamsūn	خمسون

60 sixty	sittūn	ستّون
70 seventy	sab'ūn	سبعون
80 eighty	θamānūn	ثمانون
90 ninety	tis'ūn	تسعون

100 one hundred	mi'a	مائة
200 two hundred	mi'atān	مائتان
300 three hundred	θalāθumi'a	ثلاثمائة
400 four hundred	rub'umi'a	أربعمائة
500 five hundred	χamsumi'a	خمسمائة

600 six hundred	sittumi'a	ستّمائة
700 seven hundred	sab'umi'a	سبعمائة
800 eight hundred	θamānimi'a	ثمانمائة
900 nine hundred	tis'umi'a	تسعمائة
1000 one thousand	alf	ألف

| 10000 ten thousand | 'aʃarat 'ālāf | عشرة آلاف |
| one hundred thousand | mi'at alf | مائة ألف |

| million | milyūn (m) | مليون |
| billion | milyār (m) | مليار |

3. Humans. Family

man (adult male)	raʒul (m)	رجل
young man	ʃābb (m)	شابّ
teenager	murāhiq (m)	مراهق
woman	imra'a (f)	إمرأة
girl (young woman)	fatāt (f)	فتاة

age	'umr (m)	عمر
adult (adj)	bāliɣ (m)	بالغ
middle-aged (adj)	fi muntaşaf al 'umr	في منتصف العمر
elderly (adj)	'aʒūz	عجوز
old (adj)	'aʒūz	عجوز

old man	'aʒūz (m)	عجوز
old woman	'aʒūza (f)	عجوزة
retirement	ma'āʃ (m)	معاش
to retire (from job)	uḥīl 'alal ma'āʃ	أحيل على المعاش
retiree	mutaqā'id (m)	متقاعد

English	Transliteration	Arabic
mother	umm (f)	أُمّ
father	ab (m)	أب
son	ibn (m)	إبن
daughter	ibna (f)	إبنة
brother	aχ (m)	أخ
elder brother	al aχ al kabīr (m)	الأخ الكبير
younger brother	al aχ aṣ ṣayīr (m)	الأخ الصغير
sister	uχt (f)	أخت
elder sister	al uχt al kabīra (f)	الأخت الكبيرة
younger sister	al uχt aṣ ṣayīra (f)	الأخت الصغيرة
parents	wālidān (du)	والدان
child	ṭifl (m)	طفل
children	aṭfāl (pl)	أطفال
stepmother	zawʒat al ab (f)	زوجة الأب
stepfather	zawʒ al umm (m)	زوج الأمّ
grandmother	ʒidda (f)	جدّة
grandfather	ʒadd (m)	جدّ
grandson	ḥafīd (m)	حفيد
granddaughter	ḥafīda (f)	حفيدة
grandchildren	aḥfād (pl)	أحفاد
uncle	'amm (m), χāl (m)	عمّ، خال
aunt	'amma (f), χāla (f)	عمّة، خالة
nephew	ibn al aχ (m), ibn al uχt (m)	إبن الأخ، إبن الأخت
niece	ibnat al aχ (f), ibnat al uχt (f)	إبنة الأخ، إبنة الأخت
wife	zawʒa (f)	زوجة
husband	zawʒ (m)	زوج
married (masc.)	mutazawwiʒ	متزوّج
married (fem.)	mutazawwiʒa	متزوّجة
widow	armala (f)	أرملة
widower	armal (m)	أرمل
name (first name)	ism (m)	إسم
surname (last name)	ism al 'ā'ila (m)	إسم العائلة
relative	qarīb (m)	قريب
friend (masc.)	ṣadīq (m)	صديق
friendship	ṣadāqa (f)	صداقة
partner	rafīq (m)	رفيق
superior (n)	ra'īs (m)	رئيس
colleague	zamīl (m)	زميل
neighbors	ʒirān (pl)	جيران

4. Human body

organism (body)	ʒism (m)	جسم
body	ʒism (m)	جسم

heart	qalb (m)	قلب
blood	dam (m)	دم
brain	muχχ (m)	مخ
nerve	'aṣab (m)	عصب
bone	'aẓm (m)	عظم
skeleton	haykal 'aẓmiy (m)	هيكل عظميّ
spine (backbone)	'amūd faqriy (m)	عمود فقريّ
rib	ḍil' (m)	ضلع
skull	ʒumʒuma (f)	جمجمة
muscle	'aḍala (f)	عضلة
lungs	ri'atān (du)	رئتان
skin	buʃra (m)	بشرة
head	ra's (m)	رأس
face	waʒh (m)	وجه
nose	anf (m)	أنف
forehead	ʒabha (f)	جبهة
cheek	χadd (m)	خد
mouth	fam (m)	فم
tongue	lisān (m)	لسان
tooth	sinn (f)	سنّ
lips	ʃifāh (pl)	شفاه
chin	ðaqan (m)	ذقن
ear	uðun (f)	أذن
neck	raqaba (f)	رقبة
throat	ḥalq (m)	حلق
eye	'ayn (f)	عين
pupil	ḥadaqa (f)	حدقة
eyebrow	ḥāʒib (m)	حاجب
eyelash	rimʃ (m)	رمش
hair	ʃa'r (m)	شعر
hairstyle	tasrīḥa (f)	تسريحة
mustache	ʃawārib (pl)	شوارب
beard	liḥya (f)	لحية
to have (a beard, etc.)	'indahu	عنده
bald (adj)	aṣla'	أصلع
hand	yad (m)	يد
arm	ðirā' (f)	ذراع
finger	iṣba' (m)	إصبع
nail	ẓufr (m)	ظفر
palm	kaff (f)	كفّ
shoulder	katf (f)	كتف
leg	riʒl (f)	رجل
foot	qadam (f)	قدم

| knee | rukba (f) | ركبة |
| heel | ʻaqb (m) | عقب |

back	ẓahr (m)	ظهر
waist	χaṣr (m)	خصر
beauty mark	ʃāma (f)	شامة
birthmark (café au lait spot)	waḥma	وحمة

5. Medicine. Diseases. Drugs

health	ṣiḥḥa (f)	صحّة
well (not sick)	salīm	سليم
sickness	maraḍ (m)	مرض
to be sick	maraḍ	مرض
ill, sick (adj)	marīḍ	مريض

cold (illness)	bard (m)	برد
to catch a cold	aṣābahu al bard	أصابه البرد
tonsillitis	iltihāb al lawzatayn (m)	التهاب اللوزتين
pneumonia	iltihāb ar ri'atayn (m)	إلتهاب الرئتين
flu, influenza	inflūnza (f)	إنفلونزا

runny nose (coryza)	zukām (m)	زكام
cough	suʻāl (m)	سعال
to cough (vi)	saʻal	سعل
to sneeze (vi)	ʻaṭas	عطس

stroke	sakta (f)	سكتة
heart attack	iḥtiʃā' (m)	إحتشاء
allergy	ḥassāsiyya (f)	حسّاسيّة
asthma	rabw (m)	ربو
diabetes	ad dā' as sukkariy (m)	الداء السكّريَ

tumor	waram (m)	ورم
cancer	saraṭān (m)	سرطان
alcoholism	idmān al χamr (m)	إدمان الخمر
AIDS	al aydz (m)	الايدز
fever	ḥumma (f)	حمّى
seasickness	duwār al baḥr (m)	دوار البحر

bruise (hématome)	kadma (f)	كدمة
bump (lump)	tawarrum (m)	تورّم
to limp (vi)	ʻaraʒ	عرج
dislocation	χalʻ (m)	خلع
to dislocate (vt)	χalaʻ	خلع

fracture	kasr (m)	كسر
burn (injury)	ḥarq (m)	حرق
injury	iṣāba (f)	إصابة

| pain, ache | alam (m) | ألم |
| toothache | alam al asnān (m) | ألم الأسنان |

to sweat (perspire)	'ariq	عرق
deaf (adj)	aṭraʃ	أطرش
mute (adj)	axras	أخرس

immunity	manā'a (f)	مناعة
virus	virūs (m)	فيروس
microbe	mikrūb (m)	ميكروب
bacterium	ʒurθūma (f)	جرثومة
infection	'adwa (f)	عدوى

hospital	mustaʃfa (m)	مستشفى
cure	'ilāʒ (m)	علاج
to vaccinate (vt)	laqqaḥ	لقّح
to be in a coma	kān fi ḥālat ɣaybūba	كان في حالة غيبوبة
intensive care	al 'ināya al murakkaza (f)	العناية المركّزة
symptom	'araḍ (m)	عرض
pulse	nabḍ (m)	نبض

6. Feelings. Emotions. Conversation

I, me	ana	أنا
you (masc.)	anta	أنت
you (fem.)	anti	أنت
he	huwa	هو
she	hiya	هي

we	naḥnu	نحن
you (to a group)	antum	أنتم
they	hum	هم
Hello! (form.)	as salāmu 'alaykum!	السلام عليكم!
Good morning!	ṣabāḥ al xayr!	صباح الخير!
Good afternoon!	nahārak sa'īd!	نهارك سعيد!
Good evening!	masā' al xayr!	مساء الخير!

to say hello	sallam	سلّم
to greet (vt)	sallam 'ala	سلّم على
How are you?	kayfa ḥāluka?	كيف حالك؟
Bye-Bye! Goodbye!	ma' as salāma!	مع السلامة!
Thank you!	ʃukran!	شكرًا!

feelings	maʃā'ir (pl)	مشاعر
to be hungry	arād an ya'kul	أراد أن يأكل
to be thirsty	arād an yaʃrab	أراد أن يشرب
tired (adj)	ta'bān	تعبان

| to be worried | qalaq | قلق |
| to be nervous | qalaq | قلق |

| hope | amal (m) | أمل |
| to hope (vi, vt) | tamanna | تمنّى |

character	ṭab' (m)	طبع
modest (adj)	mutawāḍi'	متواضع
lazy (adj)	kaslān	كسلان
generous (adj)	karīm	كريم
talented (adj)	mawhūb	موهوب

honest (adj)	amīn	أمين
serious (adj)	ʒādd	جادّ
shy, timid (adj)	χaʒūl	خجول
sincere (adj)	muχliṣ	مخلص
coward	ʒabān (m)	جبان

to sleep (vi)	nām	نام
dream	ḥulm (m)	حلم
bed	sarīr (m)	سرير
pillow	wisāda (f)	وسادة

insomnia	araq (m)	أرق
to go to bed	ðahab ila n nawm	ذهب إلى النوم
nightmare	kābūs (m)	كابوس
alarm clock	munabbih (m)	منبّه

smile	ibtisāma (f)	إبتسامة
to smile (vi)	ibtasam	إبتسم
to laugh (vi)	ḍaḥik	ضحك

quarrel	muʃāʒara (f)	مشاجرة
insult	ihāna (f)	إهانة
resentment	ḍaym (m)	ضيم
angry (mad)	za'lān	زعلان

7. Clothing. Personal accessories

clothes	malābis (pl)	ملابس
coat (overcoat)	mi'ṭaf (m)	معطف
fur coat	mi'ṭaf farw (m)	معطف فرو
jacket (e.g., leather ~)	ʒākīt (m)	جاكيت
raincoat (trenchcoat, etc.)	mi'ṭaf lil maṭar (m)	معطف للمطر

shirt (button shirt)	qamīṣ (m)	قميص
pants	banṭalūn (m)	بنطلون
suit jacket	sutra (f)	سترة
suit	badla (f)	بدلة

dress (frock)	fustān (m)	فستان
skirt	tannūra (f)	تنّورة
T-shirt	ti ʃirt (m)	تي شيرت

bathrobe	θawb ḥammām (m)	ثوب حمّام
pajamas	biʒāma (f)	بيجاما
workwear	θiyāb al 'amal (m)	ثياب العمل
underwear	malābis dāxiliyya (pl)	ملابس داخليّة
socks	ʒawārib (pl)	جوارب
bra	ḥammālat ṣadr (f)	حمّالة صدر
pantyhose	ʒawārib kulūn (pl)	جوارب كولون
stockings (thigh highs)	ʒawārib nisā'iyya (pl)	جوارب نسائية
bathing suit	libās sibāḥa (m)	لباس سباحة
hat	qubba'a (f)	قبّعة
footwear	aḥðiya (pl)	أحذية
boots (e.g., cowboy ~)	būt (m)	بوت
heel	ka'b (m)	كعب
shoestring	ʃarīṭ (m)	شريط
shoe polish	warnīʃ al ḥiðā' (m)	ورنيش الحذاء
cotton (n)	quṭn (m)	قطن
wool (n)	ṣūf (m)	صوف
fur (n)	farw (m)	فرو
gloves	quffāz (m)	قفّاز
mittens	quffāz muɣlaq (m)	قفّاز مغلق
scarf (muffler)	'iʃārb (m)	إيشارب
glasses (eyeglasses)	naẓẓāra (f)	نظّارة
umbrella	ʃamsiyya (f)	شمسيّة
tie (necktie)	karavatta (f)	كرافتة
handkerchief	mandīl (m)	منديل
comb	miʃṭ (m)	مشط
hairbrush	furʃat ʃa'r (f)	فرشة شعر
buckle	bukla (f)	بكلة
belt	ḥizām (m)	حزام
purse	ʃanṭat yad (f)	شنطة يد
collar	yāqa (f)	ياقة
pocket	ʒayb (m)	جيب
sleeve	kumm (m)	كمّ
fly (on trousers)	lisān (m)	لسان
zipper (fastener)	zimām munzaliq (m)	زمام منزلق
button	zirr (m)	زرّ
to get dirty (vi)	tawassax	توسّخ
stain (mark, spot)	buq'a (f)	بقعة

8. City. Urban institutions

store	maḥall (m)	محلّ
shopping mall	markaz tiʒāriy (m)	مركز تجاريّ

supermarket	subirmarkit (m)	سوبرماركت
shoe store	maḥall aḥðiya (m)	محلّ أحذية
bookstore	maḥall kutub (m)	محلّ كتب

drugstore, pharmacy	ṣaydaliyya (f)	صيدليّة
bakery	maxbaz (m)	مخبز
pastry shop	dukkān ḥalawāniy (m)	دكّان حلوانيّ
grocery store	baqqāla (f)	بقّالة
butcher shop	malḥama (f)	ملحمة
produce store	dukkān xuḍār (m)	دكّان خضار
market	sūq (f)	سوق

hair salon	ṣālūn ḥilāqa (m)	صالون حلاقة
post office	maktab al barīd (m)	مكتب البريد
dry cleaners	tanẓīf ʒāff (m)	تنظيف جافّ
circus	sirk (m)	سيرك
zoo	ḥadīqat al ḥayawān (f)	حديقة حيوان

theater	masraḥ (m)	مسرح
movie theater	sinima (f)	سينما
museum	matḥaf (m)	متحف
library	maktaba (f)	مكتبة

mosque	masʒid (m)	مسجد
synagogue	kanīs maʿbad yahūdiy (m)	كنيس معبد يهوديّ
cathedral	katidrāʾiyya (f)	كاتدرائية
temple	maʿbad (m)	معبد
church	kanīsa (f)	كنيسة

college	kulliyya (m)	كلّيّة
university	ʒāmiʿa (f)	جامعة
school	madrasa (f)	مدرسة

hotel	funduq (m)	فندق
bank	bank (m)	بنك
embassy	safāra (f)	سفارة
travel agency	ʃarikat siyāḥa (f)	شركة سياحة

subway	mitru (m)	مترو
hospital	mustaʃfa (m)	مستشفى
gas station	maḥaṭṭat banzīn (f)	محطّة بنزين
parking lot	mawqif as sayyārāt (m)	موقف السيّارات

ENTRANCE	duxūl	دخول
EXIT	xurūʒ	خروج
PUSH	idfaʿ	إدفع
PULL	isḥab	إسحب
OPEN	maftūḥ	مفتوح
CLOSED	muɣlaq	مغلق

| monument | timθāl (m) | تمثال |
| fortress | qalʿa (f), ḥiṣn (m) | قلعة, حصن |

palace	qaṣr (m)	قصر
medieval (adj)	min al qurūn al wusṭa	من القرون الوسطى
ancient (adj)	qadīm	قديم
national (adj)	waṭaniy	وطنيّ
famous (monument, etc.)	maʃhūr	مشهور

9. Money. Finances

money	nuqūd (pl)	نقود
coin	qiṭʻa naqdiyya (f)	قطعة نقديّة
dollar	dulār (m)	دولار
euro	yuru (m)	يورو

ATM	ṣarrāf ʼāliy (m)	صرّاف آليّ
currency exchange	ṣarrāfa (f)	صرّافة
exchange rate	siʻr aṣ ṣarf (m)	سعر الصرف
cash	nuqūd (pl)	نقود

How much?	bikam?	بكم؟
to pay (vi, vt)	dafaʻ	دفع
payment	dafʻ (m)	دفع
change (give the ~)	al bāqi (m)	الباقي

price	siʻr (m)	سعر
discount	χaṣm (m)	خصم
cheap (adj)	raχīṣ	رخيص
expensive (adj)	ɣāli	غال

bank	bank (m)	بنك
account	ḥisāb (m)	حساب
credit card	biṭāqat iʼtimān (f)	بطاقة إئتمان
check	ʃīk (m)	شيك
to write a check	katab ʃīk	كتب شيكًا
checkbook	daftar ʃīkāt (m)	دفتر شيكات

debt	dayn (m)	دين
debtor	muðīn (m)	مدين
to lend (money)	sallaf	سلّف
to borrow (vi, vt)	istalaf	إستلف

to rent (~ a tuxedo)	istaʼʒar	إستأجر
on credit (adv)	bid dayn	بالدين
wallet	maḥfaẓat ʒīb (f)	محفظة جيب
safe	χizāna (f)	خزانة
inheritance	wirāθa (f)	وراثة
fortune (wealth)	θarwa (f)	ثروة

tax	ḍarība (f)	ضريبة
fine	ɣarāma (f)	غرامة
to fine (vt)	faraḍ ɣarāma	فرض غرامة

wholesale (adj)	al ʒumla	الجملة
retail (adj)	at taʒzi'a	التجزئة
to insure (vt)	amman	أمّن
insurance	ta'mīn (m)	تأمين

capital	ra's māl (m)	رأس مال
turnover	dawrat ra's al māl (f)	دورة رأس المال
stock (share)	sahm (m)	سهم
profit	ribḥ (m)	ربح
profitable (adj)	murbiḥ	مربح

crisis	azma (f)	أزمة
bankruptcy	iflās (m)	إفلاس
to go bankrupt	aflas	أفلس

accountant	muḥāsib (m)	محاسب
salary	murattab (m)	مرتّب
bonus (money)	'ilāwa (f)	علاوة

10. Transportation

bus	bāṣ (m)	باص
streetcar	trām (m)	ترام
trolley bus	truli bāṣ (m)	ترولي باص

to go by ...	rakib ...	...ركب
to get on (~ the bus)	rakib	ركب
to get off ...	nazil min	نزل من

stop (e.g., bus ~)	mawqif (m)	موقف
terminus	āxir mahaṭṭa (f)	آخر محطّة
schedule	ʒadwal (m)	جدول
ticket	taðkira (f)	تذكرة
to be late (for ...)	ta'axxar	تأخّر

taxi, cab	taksi (m)	تاكسي
by taxi	bit taksi	بالتاكسي
taxi stand	mawqif taksi (m)	موقف تاكسي

traffic	ḥarakat al murūr (f)	حركة المرور
rush hour	sā'at að ðurwa (f)	ساعة الذروة
to park (vi)	awqaf	أوقف

subway	mitru (m)	مترو
station	maḥaṭṭa (f)	محطّة
train	qiṭār (m)	قطار
train station	maḥaṭṭat qiṭār (f)	محطّة قطار
rails	quḍubān (pl)	قضبان
compartment	ɣurfa (f)	غرفة
berth	sarīr (m)	سرير

airplane	ṭā'ira (f)	طائرة
air ticket	taðkirat ṭā'ira (f)	تذكرة طائرة
airline	ʃarikat ṭayarān (f)	شركة طيران
airport	maṭār (m)	مطار
flight (act of flying)	ṭayarān (m)	طيران
luggage	aʃʃunaṭ (pl)	الشنط
luggage cart	'arabat ʃunaṭ (f)	عربة شنط
ship	safīna (f)	سفينة
cruise ship	bāxira siyahiyya (f)	باخرة سياحيّة
yacht	yaxt (m)	يخت
boat (flat-bottomed ~)	markab (m)	مركب
captain	qubṭān (m)	قبطان
cabin	kabīna (f)	كابينة
port (harbor)	mīnā' (m)	ميناء
bicycle	darrāʒa (f)	درّاجة
scooter	skutir (m)	سكوتر
motorcycle, bike	darrāʒa nāriyya (f)	درّاجة ناريّة
pedal	dawwāsa (f)	دوّاسة
pump	ṭulumba (f)	طلمبة
wheel	'aʒala (f)	عجلة
automobile, car	sayyāra (f)	سيّارة
ambulance	is'āf (m)	إسعاف
truck	ʃāḥina (f)	شاحنة
used (adj)	musta'mal	مستعمل
car crash	ḥādiθ sayyāra (f)	حادث سيّارة
repair	iṣlāḥ (m)	إصلاح

11. Food. Part 1

meat	laḥm (m)	لحم
chicken	daʒāʒ (m)	دجاج
duck	baṭṭa (f)	بطّة
pork	laḥm al xinzīr (m)	لحم الخنزير
veal	laḥm il 'iʒl (m)	لحم العجل
lamb	laḥm aḍ ḍa'n (m)	لحم الضأن
beef	laḥm al baqar (m)	لحم البقر
sausage (bologna, pepperoni, etc.)	suʒuq (m)	سجق
egg	bayḍa (f)	بيضة
fish	samak (m)	سمك
cheese	ʒubna (f)	جبنة
sugar	sukkar (m)	سكّر
salt	milḥ (m)	ملح

rice	urz (m)	أرز
pasta (macaroni)	makarūna (f)	مكرونة
butter	zubda (f)	زبدة
vegetable oil	zayt (m)	زيت
bread	χubz (m)	خبز
chocolate (n)	ʃukulāta (f)	شكولاتة
wine	nabīð (f)	نبيذ
coffee	qahwa (f)	قهوة
milk	ḥalīb (m)	حليب
juice	ʿaṣīr (m)	عصير
beer	bīra (f)	بيرة
tea	ʃāy (m)	شاي
tomato	ṭamāṭim (f)	طماطم
cucumber	χiyār (m)	خيار
carrot	ʒazar (m)	جزر
potato	baṭāṭis (f)	بطاطس
onion	baṣal (m)	بصل
garlic	θūm (m)	ثوم
cabbage	kurumb (m)	كرنب
beetroot	banʒar (m)	بنجر
eggplant	bātinʒān (m)	باذنجان
dill	ʃabat (m)	شبت
lettuce	χass (m)	خسّ
corn (maize)	ðura (f)	ذرَة
fruit	fākiha (f)	فاكهة
apple	tuffāḥa (f)	تفاحة
pear	kummaθra (f)	كمّثرى
lemon	laymūn (m)	ليمون
orange	burtuqāl (m)	برتقال
strawberry (garden ~)	farawla (f)	فراولة
plum	barqūq (m)	برقوق
raspberry	tūt al ʿullayq al aḥmar (m)	توت العليق الأحمر
pineapple	ananās (m)	أناناس
banana	mawz (m)	موز
watermelon	baṭṭīχ aḥmar (m)	بطيخ أحمر
grape	ʿinab (m)	عنب
melon	baṭṭīχ aṣfar (f)	بطيخ أصفر

12. Food. Part 2

cuisine	maṭbaχ (m)	مطبخ
recipe	waṣfa (f)	وصفة
food	akl (m)	أكل
to have breakfast	afṭar	أفطر
to have lunch	taɣadda	تغدّى

to have dinner	ta'aʃʃa	تعشّى
taste, flavor	ṭaʿm (m)	طعم
tasty (adj)	laðīð	لذيذ
cold (adj)	bārid	بارد
hot (adj)	sāxin	ساخن
sweet (sugary)	musakkar	مسكّر
salty (adj)	māliḥ	مالح
sandwich (bread)	sandawitʃ (m)	ساندويتش
side dish	ṭabaq ʒānibiy (m)	طبق جانبيّ
filling (for cake, pie)	ḥaʃwa (f)	حشوة
sauce	ṣalṣa (f)	صلصة
piece (of cake, pie)	qiṭʿa (f)	قطعة
diet	ḥimya ɣaðā'iyya (f)	حمية غذائية
vitamin	vitamīn (m)	فيتامين
calorie	su'ra ḥarāriyya (f)	سعرة حراريّة
vegetarian (n)	nabātiy (m)	نباتيّ
restaurant	maṭʿam (m)	مطعم
coffee house	kafé (m), maqha (m)	كافيه، مقهى
appetite	ʃahiyya (f)	شهيّة
Enjoy your meal!	hanī'an marī'an!	!هنيئًا مريئًا
waiter	nādil (m)	نادل
waitress	nādila (f)	نادلة
bartender	bārman (m)	بارمان
menu	qā'imat aṭ ṭaʿām (f)	قائمة طعام
spoon	milʿaqa (f)	ملعقة
knife	sikkīn (m)	سكّين
fork	ʃawka (f)	شوكة
cup (e.g., coffee ~)	finʒān (m)	فنجان
plate (dinner ~)	ṭabaq (m)	طبق
saucer	ṭabaq finʒān (m)	طبق فنجان
napkin (on table)	mandīl (m)	منديل
toothpick	xallat asnān (f)	خلّة أسنان
to order (meal)	ṭalab	طلب
course, dish	waʒba (f)	وجبة
portion	waʒba (f)	وجبة
appetizer	muqabbilāt (pl)	مقبّلات
salad	sulṭa (f)	سلطة
soup	ʃūrba (f)	شوربة
dessert	ḥalawiyyāt (pl)	حلويّات
jam (whole fruit jam)	murabba (m)	مربى
ice-cream	muθallaʒāt (pl)	مثلّجات
check	ḥisāb (m)	حساب
to pay the check	dafaʿ al ḥisāb	دفع الحساب
tip	baqʃīʃ (m)	بقشيش

13. House. Apartment. Part 1

English	Transliteration	Arabic
house	bayt (m)	بيت
country house	bayt rīfiy (m)	بيت ريفيّ
villa (seaside ~)	villa (f)	فيلا
floor, story	ṭābiq (m)	طابق
entrance	madχal (m)	مدخل
wall	ḥā'iṭ (m)	حائط
roof	saqf (m)	سقف
chimney	madχana (f)	مدخنة
attic (storage place)	'ullayya (f)	عليّة
window	ʃubbāk (m)	شبّاك
window ledge	raff ʃubbāk (f)	رف شبّاك
balcony	ʃurfa (f)	شرفة
stairs (stairway)	sullam (m)	سلّم
mailbox	ṣundūq al barīd (m)	صندوق البريد
garbage can	ṣundūq az zubāla (m)	صندوق الزبالة
elevator	miṣ'ad (m)	مصعد
electricity	kahrabā' (m)	كهرباء
light bulb	lamba (f)	لمبة
switch	miftāḥ (m)	مفتاح
wall socket	barizat al kahrabā' (f)	بريزة الكهرباء
fuse	fāṣima (f)	فاصمة
door	bāb (m)	باب
handle, doorknob	qabḍat al bāb (f)	قبضة الباب
key	miftāḥ (m)	مفتاح
doormat	siʒāda (f)	سجادة
door lock	qifl al bāb (m)	قفل الباب
doorbell	ʒaras (m)	جرس
knock (at the door)	ṭarq, daqq (m)	طرق، دقّ
to knock (vi)	daqq	دقّ
peephole	al 'ayn as siḥriyya (m)	العين السحريّة
yard	finā' (m)	فناء
garden	ḥadīqa (f)	حديقة
swimming pool	masbaḥ (m)	مسبح
gym (home gym)	qā'at at tamrīnāt (f)	قاعة التمرينات
tennis court	mal'ab tinis (m)	ملعب تنس
garage	qarāʒ (m)	جراج
private property	milkiyya χāṣṣa (f)	ملكيّة خاصّة
warning sign	lāfitat taḥðīr (f)	لافتة تحذير
security	ḥirāsa (f)	حراسة
security guard	ḥāris amn (m)	حارس أمن
renovations	taʒdīdāt (m)	تجديدات
to renovate (vt)	ʒaddad	جدّد

to put in order	nazzam	نظم
to paint (~ a wall)	dahan	دهن
wallpaper	waraq ḥīʼṭān (m)	ورق حيطان
to varnish (vt)	ṭala bil warnīʃ	طلى بالورنيش

pipe	māsūra (f)	ماسورة
tools	adawāt (pl)	أدوات
basement	sirdāb (m)	سرداب
sewerage (system)	ʃabakit il maʒāry (f)	شبكة مياه المجاري

14. House. Apartment. Part 2

apartment	ʃaqqa (f)	شقة
room	ɣurfa (f)	غرفة
bedroom	ɣurfat an nawm (f)	غرفة الوم
dining room	ɣurfat il akl (f)	غرفة الأكل

living room	ṣālat al istiqbāl (f)	صالة الإستقبال
study (home office)	maktab (m)	مكتب
entry room	madχal (m)	مدخل
bathroom (room with a bath or shower)	ḥammām (m)	حمّام

| half bath | ḥammām (m) | حمّام |

| floor | arḍ (f) | أرض |
| ceiling | saqf (m) | سقف |

to dust (vt)	masaḥ al ɣubār	مسح الغبار
vacuum cleaner	miknasa kahrabāʼiyya (f)	مكنسة كهربائيّة
to vacuum (vt)	nazzaf bi miknasa kahrabāʼiyya	نظف بمكنسة كهربائيّة

mop	mimsaḥa ṭawīla (f)	ممسحة طويلة
dust cloth	mimsaḥa (f)	ممسحة
short broom	miqaʃʃa (f)	مقشّة
dustpan	ʒārūf (m)	جاروف

furniture	aθāθ (m)	أثاث
table	maktab (m)	مكتب
chair	kursiy (m)	كرسيّ
armchair	kursiy (m)	كرسيّ

bookcase	χizānat kutub (f)	خزانة كتب
shelf	raff (m)	رفّ
wardrobe	dūlāb (m)	دولاب

mirror	mirʼāt (f)	مرآة
carpet	siʒāda (f)	سجادة
fireplace	midfaʼa ḥāʼiṭiyya (f)	مدفأة حائطيّة
drapes	satāʼir (pl)	ستائر

table lamp	miṣbāḥ aṭ ṭāwila (m)	مصباح الطاولة
chandelier	naᴣafa (f)	نجفة
kitchen	maṭbaχ (m)	مطبخ
gas stove (range)	butuɣāz (m)	بوتوغاز
electric stove	furn kaharabā'iy (m)	فرن كهربائيّ
microwave oven	furn al mikruwayv (m)	فرن الميكرووْيف
refrigerator	θallāᴣa (f)	ثلاجة
freezer	frīzir (m)	فريزير
dishwasher	ɣassāla (f)	غسّالة
faucet	ḥanafiyya (f)	حنفيّة
meat grinder	farrāmat laḥm (f)	فرّامة لحم
juicer	'aṣṣāra (f)	عصّارة
toaster	maḥmaṣat χubz (f)	محمصة خبز
mixer	χallāṭ (m)	خلّاط
coffee machine	mākinat ṣan' al qahwa (f)	ماكينة صنع القهوة
kettle	barrād (m)	برّاد
teapot	barrād aʃ ʃāy (m)	برّاد الشاي
TV set	tilivizyūn (m)	تليفزيون
VCR (video recorder)	ᴣihāz tasᴣīl vidiyu (m)	جهاز تسجيل فيديو
iron (e.g., steam ~)	makwāt (f)	مكواة
telephone	hātif (m)	هاتف

15. Professions. Social status

director	mudīr (m)	مدير
superior	ra'īs (m)	رئيس
president	ra'īs (m)	رئيس
assistant	musā'id (m)	مساعد
secretary	sikirtīr (m)	سكرتير
owner, proprietor	ṣāḥib (m)	صاحب
partner	ʃarīk (m)	شريك
stockholder	musāhim (m)	مساهم
businessman	raᴣul a'māl (m)	رجل أعمال
millionaire	milyunīr (m)	مليونير
billionaire	milyardīr (m)	ملياردير
actor	mumaθθil (m)	ممثّل
architect	muhandis mi'māriy (m)	مهندس معماريّ
banker	ṣāḥib maṣraf (m)	صاحب مصرف
broker	simsār (m)	سمسار
veterinarian	ṭabīb bayṭariy (m)	طبيب بيطريّ
doctor	ṭabīb (m)	طبيب

chambermaid	'āmilat tanẓīf ɣuraf (f)	عاملة تنظيف غرف
designer	muṣammim (m)	مصمّم
correspondent	murāsil (m)	مراسل
delivery man	sā'i (m)	ساع

electrician	kahrabā'iy (m)	كهربائيّ
musician	'āzif (m)	عازف
babysitter	murabbiyat aṭfāl (f)	مربّية الأطفال
hairdresser	ḥallāq (m)	حلّاق
herder, shepherd	rā'i (m)	راع

singer (masc.)	muɣanni (m)	مغنّ
translator	mutarʒim (m)	مترجم
writer	kātib (m)	كاتب
carpenter	naʒʒār (m)	نجّار
cook	ṭabbāχ (m)	طبّاخ

fireman	raʒul iṭfā' (m)	رجل إطفاء
police officer	ʃurṭiy (m)	شرطيّ
mailman	sā'i al barīd (m)	ساعي البريد
programmer	mubarmiʒ (m)	مبرمج
salesman (store staff)	bā'i' (m)	بائع

worker	'āmil (m)	عامل
gardener	bustāniy (m)	بستانيّ
plumber	sabbāk (m)	سبّاك
dentist	ṭabīb al asnān (m)	طبيب الأسنان
flight attendant (fem.)	muḍīfat ṭayarān (f)	مضيفة طيران

dancer (masc.)	rāqiṣ (m)	راقص
bodyguard	ḥāris ʃaχṣiy (m)	حارس شخصيّ
scientist	'ālim (m)	عالم
schoolteacher	mudarris madrasa (m)	مدرّس مدرسة

farmer	muzāri' (m)	مزارع
surgeon	ʒarrāḥ (m)	جرّاح
miner	'āmil manʒam (m)	عامل منجم
chef (kitchen chef)	ʃāf (m)	شاف
driver	sā'iq (m)	سائق

16. Sport

kind of sports	naw' min ar riyāḍa (m)	نوع من الرياضة
soccer	kurat al qadam (f)	كرة القدم
hockey	huki (m)	هوكي
basketball	kurat as salla (f)	كرة السلّة
baseball	kurat al qā'ida (f)	كرة القاعدة

| volleyball | al kura aṭ ṭā'ira (m) | الكرة الطائرة |
| boxing | mulākama (f) | ملاكمة |

wrestling	muṣāra'a (f)	مصارعة
tennis	tinis (m)	تنس
swimming	sibāḥa (f)	سباحة
chess	ʃaṭranʒ (m)	شطرنج
running	ʒary (m)	جري
athletics	al'āb al qiwa (pl)	ألعاب القوى
figure skating	tazalluʒ fanniy 'alal ʒalīd (m)	تزلج فنّيَ على الجليد
cycling	sibāq ad darrāʒāt (m)	سباق الدرّاجات
billiards	bilyārdu (m)	بلياردو
bodybuilding	kamāl aʒsām (m)	كمال أجسام
golf	gūlf (m)	جولف
scuba diving	al ɣawṣ taḥt al mā' (m)	الغوص تحت الماء
sailing	riyāḍa ibḥār al marākib (f)	رياضة إبحار المراكب
archery	rimāya (f)	رماية
period, half	ʃawṭ (m)	شوط
half-time	istirāḥa ma bayn aʃ ʃawṭayn (f)	إستراحة ما بين الشوطين
tie	ta'ādul (m)	تعادل
to tie (vi)	ta'ādal	تعادل
treadmill	ʒihāz al maʃy (m)	جهاز المشي
player	lā'ib (m)	لاعب
substitute	lā'ib iḥtiyāṭiy (m)	لاعب إحتياطيّ
substitutes bench	dikkat al iḥtiāṭy (f)	دكة الإحتياطي
match	mubārāt (f)	مباراة
goal	marma (m)	مرمى
goalkeeper	ḥāris al marma (m)	حارس المرمى
goal (score)	hadaf (m)	هدف
Olympic Games	al'āb ulumbiyya (pl)	ألعاب أولمبيّة
to set a record	fāz bi raqm qiyāsiy	فاز برقم قياسيّ
final	mubarāt nihā'iyya (f)	مباراة نهائيّة
champion	baṭal (m)	بطل
championship	buṭūla (f)	بطولة
winner	fā'iz (m)	فائز
victory	fawz (m)	فوز
to win (vi)	fāz	فاز
to lose (not win)	xasir	خسر
medal	midāliyya (f)	ميداليّة
first place	al martaba al ūla (f)	المرتبة الأولى
second place	al martaba aθ θāniya (f)	المرتبة الثانية
third place	al martaba aθ θāliθa (f)	المرتبة الثالثة
stadium	mal'ab (m)	ملعب
fan, supporter	muʃaʒʒi' (m)	مشجّع

trainer, coach	mudarrib (m)	مدرّب
training	tadrīb (m)	تدريب

17. Foreign languages. Orthography

language	luɣa (f)	لغة
to study (vt)	daras	درس
pronunciation	nuṭq (m)	نطق
accent	lukna (f)	لكنة
noun	ism (m)	إسم
adjective	ṣifa (f)	صفة
verb	fi'l (m)	فعل
adverb	ẓarf (m)	ظرف
pronoun	ḍamīr (m)	ضمير
interjection	ḥarf nidā' (m)	حرف نداء
preposition	ḥarf al ʒarr (m)	حرف الجرّ
root	ʒiðr al kalima (m)	جذر الكلمة
ending	nihāya (f)	نهاية
prefix	sābiqa (f)	سابقة
syllable	maqṭaʻ lafẓiy (m)	مقطع لفظيّ
suffix	lāḥiqa (f)	لاحقة
stress mark	nabra (f)	نبرة
period, dot	nuqṭa (f)	نقطة
comma	fāṣila (f)	فاصلة
colon	nuqṭatān ra'siyyatān (du)	نقطتان رأسيتان
ellipsis	θalāθ nuqaṭ (pl)	ثلاث نقط
question	su'āl (m)	سؤال
question mark	'alāmat istifhām (f)	علامة إستفهام
exclamation point	'alāmat ta'aʒʒub (f)	علامة تعجّب
in quotation marks	bayn 'alāmatay al iqtibās	بين علامتي الإقتباس
in parenthesis	bayn al qawsayn	بين القوسين
letter	ḥarf (m)	حرف
capital letter	ḥarf kabīr (m)	حرف كبير
sentence	ʒumla (f)	جملة
group of words	maʒmū'a min al kalimāt (pl)	مجموعة من الكلمات
expression	'ibāra (f)	عبارة
subject	fā'il (m)	فاعل
predicate	musnad (m)	مسند
line	saṭr (m)	سطر
paragraph	fiqra (f)	فقرة
synonym	murādif (m)	مرادف
antonym	mutaḍādd luɣawiy (m)	متضادّ

exception	istiθnā' (m)	إستثناء
to underline (vt)	waḍa' xaṭṭ taḥt	وضع خطًا تحت

rules	qawā'id (pl)	قواعد
grammar	an naḥw waṣ ṣarf (m)	النحو والصرف
vocabulary	mufradāt al luɣa (pl)	مفردات اللغة
phonetics	ṣawtīyyāt (pl)	صوتيًات
alphabet	alifbā' (m)	الفباء

textbook	kitāb ta'līm (m)	كتاب تعليم
dictionary	qāmūs (m)	قاموس
phrasebook	kitāb lil 'ibārāt aʃ ʃā'i'a (m)	كتاب للعبارت الشائعة

word	kalima (f)	كلمة
meaning	ma'na (m)	معنى
memory	ðākira (f)	ذاكرة

18. The Earth. Geography

the Earth	al arḍ (f)	الأرض
the globe (the Earth)	al kura al arḍiyya (f)	الكرة الأرضيّة
planet	kawkab (m)	كوكب

geography	ʒuɣrāfiya (f)	جغرافيا
nature	ṭabī'a (f)	طبيعة
map	xarīṭa (f)	خريطة
atlas	aṭlas (m)	أطلس

in the north	fiʃ ʃimāl	في الشمال
in the south	fil ʒanūb	في الجنوب
in the west	fil ɣarb	في الغرب
in the east	fiʃ ʃarq	في الشرق

sea	baḥr (m)	بحر
ocean	muḥīṭ (m)	محيط
gulf (bay)	xalīʒ (m)	خليج
straits	maḍīq (m)	مضيق

continent (mainland)	qārra (f)	قارّة
island	ʒazīra (f)	جزيرة
peninsula	ʃibh ʒazīra (f)	شبه جزيرة
archipelago	maʒmū'at ʒuzur (f)	مجموعة جزر

harbor	mīnā' (m)	ميناء
coral reef	ʃi'āb marʒāniyya (pl)	شعاب مرجانيّة
shore	sāḥil (m)	ساحل
coast	sāḥil (m)	ساحل

flow (flood tide)	madd (m)	مدّ
ebb (ebb tide)	ʒazr (m)	جزر

latitude	'arḍ (m)	عرض
longitude	ṭūl (m)	طول
parallel	mutawāzi (m)	متواز
equator	ẋaṭṭ al istiwā' (m)	خط الإستواء

sky	samā' (f)	سماء
horizon	ufuq (m)	أفق
atmosphere	al ɣilāf al ʒawwiy (m)	الغلاف الجوّيّ

mountain	ʒabal (m)	جبل
summit, top	qimma (f)	قمّة
cliff	ʒurf (m)	جرف
hill	tall (m)	تلّ

volcano	burkān (m)	بركان
glacier	nahr ʒalīdiy (m)	نهر جليديّ
waterfall	ʃallāl (m)	شلّال
plain	sahl (m)	سهل

river	nahr (m)	نهر
spring (natural source)	'ayn (m)	عين
bank (of river)	ḍiffa (f)	ضفّة
downstream (adv)	f ittiʒāh maʒra an nahr	في إتجاه مجرى النهر
upstream (adv)	ḍidd at tayyār	ضد التيّار

lake	buḥayra (f)	بحيرة
dam	sadd (m)	سدّ
canal	qanāt (f)	قناة
swamp (marshland)	mustanqa' (m)	مستنقع
ice	ʒalīd (m)	جليد

19. Countries of the world. Part 1

Europe	urūbba (f)	أوروبّا
European Union	al ittiḥād al urubbiy (m)	الإتّحاد الأوروبّيّ
European (n)	urūbbiy (m)	أوروبّيّ
European (adj)	urūbbiy	أوروبّي

Austria	an nimsa (f)	النمسا
Great Britain	briṭāniya al 'uẓma (f)	بريطانيا العظمى
England	inʒiltirra (f)	إنجلترًا
Belgium	balʒīka (f)	بلجيكا
Germany	almāniya (f)	ألمانيا

Netherlands	hulanda (f)	هولندا
Holland	hulanda (f)	هولندا
Greece	al yūnān (f)	اليونان
Denmark	ad danimārk (f)	الدانمارك
Ireland	irlanda (f)	أيرلندا
Iceland	'āyslanda (f)	آيسلندا

Spain	isbāniya (f)	إسبانيا
Italy	iṭāliya (f)	إيطاليا
Cyprus	qubruṣ (f)	قبرص
Malta	malṭa (f)	مالطا

Norway	an nirwīʒ (f)	النرويج
Portugal	al burtuɣāl (f)	البرتغال
Finland	finlanda (f)	فنلندا
France	faransa (f)	فرنسا
Sweden	as suwayd (f)	السويد

Switzerland	swīsra (f)	سويسرا
Scotland	iskutlanda (f)	اسكتلندا
Vatican	al vatikān (m)	الفاتيكان
Liechtenstein	liʃtinʃtāyn (m)	ليشتنشتاين
Luxembourg	luksimburɣ (f)	لوكسمبورغ

Monaco	munāku (f)	موناكو
Albania	albāniya (f)	ألبانيا
Bulgaria	bulɣāriya (f)	بلغاريا
Hungary	al maʒar (f)	المجر
Latvia	lātviya (f)	لاتفيا

Lithuania	litwāniya (f)	ليتوانيا
Poland	bulanda (f)	بولندا
Romania	rumāniya (f)	رومانيا
Serbia	ṣirbiya (f)	صربيا
Slovakia	sluvākiya (f)	سلوفاكيا

Croatia	kruātiya (f)	كرواتيا
Czech Republic	atʃ tʃik (f)	التشيك
Estonia	istūniya (f)	إستونيا
Bosnia and Herzegovina	al busna wal hirsuk (f)	البوسنة والهرسك
Macedonia (Republic of ~)	maqdūniya (f)	مقدونيا

Slovenia	sluvīniya (f)	سلوفينيا
Montenegro	al ʒabal al aswad (m)	الجبل الأسود
Belarus	bilarūs (f)	بيلاروس
Moldova, Moldavia	muldāviya (f)	مولدافيا
Russia	rūsiya (f)	روسيا
Ukraine	ukrāniya (f)	أوكرانيا

20. Countries of the world. Part 2

Asia	'āsiya (f)	آسيا
Vietnam	vitnām (f)	فيتنام
India	al hind (f)	الهند
Israel	isrā'īl (f)	إسرائيل
China	aṣ ṣīn (f)	الصين
Lebanon	lubnān (f)	لبنان

Mongolia	manɣūliya (f)	منغوليا
Malaysia	malīziya (f)	ماليزيا
Pakistan	bakistān (f)	باكستان
Saudi Arabia	as sa'ūdiyya (f)	السعوديّة

Thailand	taylānd (f)	تايلاند
Taiwan	taywān (f)	تايوان
Turkey	turkiya (f)	تركيا
Japan	al yabān (f)	اليابان
Afghanistan	afɣanistān (f)	أفغانستان

Bangladesh	banʒladīʃ (f)	بنجلاديش
Indonesia	indunīsiya (f)	إندونيسيا
Jordan	al urdun (m)	الأردن
Iraq	al 'irāq (m)	العراق
Iran	ĩrān (f)	إيران

Cambodia	kambūdya (f)	كمبوديا
Kuwait	al kuwayt (f)	الكويت
Laos	lawus (f)	لاوس
Myanmar	myanmār (f)	ميانمار
Nepal	nibāl (f)	نيبال

United Arab Emirates	al imārāt al 'arabiyya al muttaḥida (pl)	الإمارات العربيّة المتّحدة
Syria	sūriya (f)	سوريا
Palestine	filisṭīn (f)	فلسطين
South Korea	kuriya al ʒanūbiyya (f)	كوريا الجنوبيّة
North Korea	kūria aʃ ʃimāliyya (f)	كوريا الشماليّة

United States of America	al wilāyāt al muttaḥida al amrīkiyya (pl)	الولايات المتّحدة الأمريكيّة
Canada	kanada (f)	كندا
Mexico	al maksīk (f)	المكسيك
Argentina	arʒantīn (f)	الأرجنتين
Brazil	al brazīl (f)	البرازيل

Colombia	kulumbiya (f)	كولومبيا
Cuba	kūba (f)	كوبا
Chile	tʃīli (f)	تشيلي
Venezuela	vinizwiyla (f)	فنزويلا
Ecuador	al iqwadūr (f)	الإكوادور

The Bahamas	ʒuzur bahāmas (pl)	جزر باهاماس
Panama	banama (f)	بنما
Egypt	miṣr (f)	مصر
Morocco	al maɣrib (m)	المغرب
Tunisia	tūnis (f)	تونس
Kenya	kiniya (f)	كينيا
Libya	lībiya (f)	ليبيا
South Africa	ʒumhūriyyat afrīqiya al ʒanūbiyya (f)	جمهريّة أفريقيا الجنوبيّة

| Australia | usturāliya (f) | أستراليا |
| New Zealand | nyu zilanda (f) | نيوزيلندا |

21. Weather. Natural disasters

weather	ṭaqs (m)	طقس
weather forecast	naʃra ʒawwiyya (f)	نشرة جوّيّة
temperature	ḥarāra (f)	حرارة
thermometer	tirmūmitr (m)	ترمومتر
barometer	barūmitr (m)	بارومتر

sun	ʃams (f)	شمس
to shine (vi)	aḍā'	أضاء
sunny (day)	muʃmis	مشمس
to come up (vi)	ʃaraq	شرق
to set (vi)	ɣarab	غرب

rain	maṭar (m)	مطر
it's raining	innaha tamṭur	إنّها تمطر
pouring rain	maṭar munhamir (f)	مطر منهمر
rain cloud	saḥābat maṭar (f)	سحابة مطر
puddle	birka (f)	بركة
to get wet (in rain)	ibtall	إبتلّ

thunderstorm	'āṣifa ra'diyya (f)	عاصفة رعديّة
lightning (~ strike)	barq (m)	برق
to flash (vi)	baraq	برق
thunder	ra'd (m)	رعد
it's thundering	tar'ad as samā'	ترعد السماء
hail	maṭar bard (m)	مطر برد
it's hailing	tamṭur as samā' bardan	تمطر السماء بردًا

heat (extreme ~)	ḥarāra (f)	حرارة
it's hot	al ʒaww ḥārr	الجوّ حارّ
it's warm	al ʒaww dāfi'	الجوّ دافئ
it's cold	al ʒaww bārid	الجوّ بارد

fog (mist)	ḍabāb (m)	ضباب
foggy	muḍabbab	مضبّب
cloud	saḥāba (f)	سحابة
cloudy (adj)	ɣā'im	غائم
humidity	ruṭūba (f)	رطوبة

snow	θalʒ (m)	ثلج
it's snowing	innaha taθluʒ	إنّها تثلج
frost (severe ~, freezing cold)	ṣaqī' (m)	صقيع
below zero (adv)	taḥt aṣ ṣifr	تحت الصفر
hoarfrost	ṣaqī' (m)	صقيع
bad weather	ṭaqs sayyi' (m)	طقس سيّء

disaster	kāriθa (f)	كارثة
flood, inundation	fayaḍān (m)	فيضان
avalanche	inhiyār θalʒiy (m)	إنهيار ثلجيّ
earthquake	zilzāl (m)	زلزال

tremor, quake	hazza arḍiyya (f)	هزّة أرضيّة
epicenter	markaz az zilzāl (m)	مركز الزلزال
eruption	θawrān (m)	ثوران
lava	ḥumam burkāniyya (pl)	حمم بركانيّة

twister, tornado	iʻṣār (m)	إعصار
hurricane	iʻṣār (m)	إعصار
tsunami	tsunāmi (m)	تسونامي
cyclone	iʻṣār (m)	إعصار

22. Animals. Part 1

animal	ḥayawān (m)	حيوان
predator	ḥayawān muftaris (m)	حيوان مفترس

tiger	namir (m)	نمر
lion	asad (m)	أسد
wolf	ðiʼb (m)	ذئب
fox	θaʻlab (m)	ثعلب
jaguar	namir amrīkiy (m)	نمر أمريكيّ

lynx	waʃaq (m)	وشق
coyote	qayūṭ (m)	قيوط
jackal	ibn ʼāwa (m)	ابن آوى
hyena	ḍabuʻ (m)	ضبع

squirrel	sinʒāb (m)	سنجاب
hedgehog	qumfuð (m)	قنفذ
rabbit	arnab (m)	أرنب
raccoon	rākūn (m)	راكون

hamster	qidād (m)	قداد
mole	χuld (m)	خلد
mouse	faʼr (m)	فأر
rat	ʒurað (m)	جرذ
bat	χuffāʃ (m)	خفاش

beaver	qundus (m)	قندس
horse	ḥiṣān (m)	حصان
deer	ayyil (m)	أيّل
camel	ʒamal (m)	جمل
zebra	ḥimār zarad (m)	حمار زرد

whale	ḥūt (m)	حوت
seal	fuqma (f)	فقمة

walrus	faẓẓ (m)	فظّ
dolphin	dilfīn (m)	دلفين
bear	dubb (m)	دبّ
monkey	qird (m)	قرد
elephant	fīl (m)	فيل
rhinoceros	χartīt (m)	خرتيت
giraffe	zarāfa (f)	زرافة
hippopotamus	faras an nahr (m)	فرس النهر
kangaroo	kanɣar (m)	كنغر
cat	qiṭṭa (f)	قطّة
dog	kalb (m)	كلب
cow	baqara (f)	بقرة
bull	θawr (m)	ثور
sheep (ewe)	χarūf (f)	خروف
goat	mā'iz (m)	ماعز
donkey	ḥimār (m)	حمار
pig, hog	χinzīr (m)	خنزير
hen (chicken)	daʒāʒa (f)	دجاجة
rooster	dīk (m)	ديك
duck	baṭṭa (f)	بطّة
goose	iwazza (f)	إوزّة
turkey (hen)	daʒāʒ rūmiy (m)	دجاج رومّي
sheepdog	kalb ra'y (m)	كلب رعي

23. Animals. Part 2

bird	ṭā'ir (m)	طائر
pigeon	ḥamāma (f)	حمامة
sparrow	'uṣfūr (m)	عصفور
tit (great tit)	qurquf (m)	قرقف
magpie	'aq'aq (m)	عقعق
eagle	nasr (m)	نسر
hawk	bāz (m)	باز
falcon	ṣaqr (m)	صقر
swan	timma (m)	تمّة
crane	kurkiy (m)	كركي
stork	laqlaq (m)	لقلق
parrot	babaɣā' (m)	بيغاء
peacock	ṭāwūs (m)	طاووس
ostrich	na'āma (f)	نعامة
heron	balaʃūn (m)	بلشون
nightingale	bulbul (m)	بلبل

swallow	sunūnū (m)	سنونو
woodpecker	naqqār al χaʃab (m)	نقّار الخشب
cuckoo	waqwāq (m)	وقواق
owl	būma (f)	بومة
penguin	biṭrīq (m)	بطريق
tuna	tūna (f)	تونة
trout	salmūn muraqqaṭ (m)	سلمون مرقّط
eel	ḥankalīs (m)	حنكليس
shark	qirʃ (m)	قرش
crab	salṭa'ūn (m)	سلطعون
jellyfish	qindīl al baḥr (m)	قنديل البحر
octopus	uχṭubūṭ (m)	أخطبوط
starfish	naʒmat al baḥr (f)	نجمة البحر
sea urchin	qumfuð al baḥr (m)	قنفذ البحر
seahorse	ḥiṣān al baḥr (m)	فرس البحر
shrimp	ʒambari (m)	جمبري
snake	θu'bān (m)	ثعبان
viper	af'a (f)	أفعى
lizard	siḥliyya (f)	سحليّة
iguana	iɣwāna (f)	إغوانة
chameleon	ḥirbā' (f)	حرباء
scorpion	'aqrab (m)	عقرب
turtle	sulaḥfāt (f)	سلحفاة
frog	ḍifḍa' (m)	ضفدع
crocodile	timsāḥ (m)	تمساح
insect, bug	ḥaʃara (f)	حشرة
butterfly	farāʃa (f)	فراشة
ant	namla (f)	نملة
fly	ðubāba (f)	ذبابة
mosquito	namūsa (f)	ناموسة
beetle	χunfusa (f)	خنفسة
bee	naḥla (f)	نحلة
spider	'ankabūt (m)	عنكبوت

24. Trees. Plants

tree	ʃaʒara (f)	شجرة
birch	batūla (f)	بتولا
oak	ballūṭ (f)	بلّوط
linden tree	ʃaʒarat zayzafūn (f)	شجرة زيزفون
aspen	ḥawr raʒrāʒ (m)	حور رجراج
maple	qayqab (f)	قيقب
spruce	ratinaʒ (f)	راتينج

pine	ṣanawbar (f)	صنوبر
cedar	arz (f)	أرز
poplar	ḥawr (f)	حور
rowan	ɣubayrā' (f)	غبيراء
beech	zān (m)	زان
elm	dardār (f)	دردار
ash (tree)	marān (f)	مران
chestnut	kastanā' (f)	كستناء
palm tree	naχla (f)	نخلة
bush	ʃuʒayra (f)	شجيرة
mushroom	fuṭr (f)	فطر
poisonous mushroom	fuṭr sāmm (m)	فطر سامّ
cep (Boletus edulis)	fuṭr bulīṭ ma'kūl (m)	فطر بوليط مأكول
russula	fuṭr russūla (m)	فطر روسّولا
fly agaric	fuṭr amānīt aṭ ṭā'ir as sāmm (m)	فطر أمانيت الطائر السامّ
death cap	fuṭr amānīt falusyāniy as sāmm (m)	فطر أمانيت فالوسياني السامّ
flower	zahra (f)	زهرة
bouquet (of flowers)	bāqat zuhūr (f)	باقة زهور
rose (flower)	warda (f)	وردة
tulip	tulīb (f)	توليب
carnation	qurumful (m)	قرنفل
camomile	babunʒ (m)	بابونج
cactus	ṣabbār (m)	صبّار
lily of the valley	sawsan al wādi (m)	سوسن الوادي
snowdrop	zahrat al laban (f)	زهرة اللبن
water lily	nilūfar (m)	نيلوفر
greenhouse (tropical ~)	dafī'a (f)	دفيئة
lawn	'uʃb (m)	عشب
flowerbed	ʒunaynat zuhūr (f)	جنينة زهور
plant	nabāt (m)	نبات
grass	'uʃb (m)	عشب
leaf	waraqa (f)	ورقة
petal	waraqat az zahra (f)	ورقة الزهرة
stem	sāq (f)	ساق
young plant (shoot)	nabta saɣīra (f)	نبتة صغيرة
cereal crops	maḥāṣīl al ḥubūb (pl)	محاصيل الحبوب
wheat	qamḥ (m)	قمح
rye	ʒāwdār (m)	جاودار
oats	ʃūfān (m)	شوفان
millet	duχn (m)	دخن
barley	ʃa'īr (m)	شعير

| corn | ðura (f) | ذرة |
| rice | urz (m) | أرز |

25. Various useful words

balance (of situation)	tawãzun (m)	توازن
base (basis)	asãs (m)	أساس
beginning	bidãya (f)	بداية
category	fi'a (f)	فئة

choice	iχtiyãr (m)	إختيار
coincidence	ṣudfa (f)	صدفة
comparison	muqãrana (f)	مقارنة
degree (extent, amount)	daraӡa (f)	درجة

development	tanmiya (f)	تنمية
difference	farq (m)	فرق
effect (e.g., of drugs)	ta'θīr (m)	تأثير
effort (exertion)	ӡuhd (m)	جهد

element	'unṣur (m)	عنصر
example (illustration)	miθãl (m)	مثال
fact	ḥaqīqa (f)	حقيقة
help	musã'ada (f)	مساعدة

ideal	miθãl (m)	مثال
kind (sort, type)	naw' (m)	نوع
mistake, error	χaṭa' (m)	خطأ
moment	laḥẓa (f)	لحظة

obstacle	'aqba (f)	عقبة
part (~ of sth)	ӡuz' (m)	جزء
pause (break)	istirãḥa (f)	إستراحة
position	mawqif (m)	موقف

problem	muʃkila (f)	مشكلة
process	'amaliyya (f)	عمليّة
progress	taqaddum (m)	تقدّم
property (quality)	χaṣṣa (f)	خاصّة

reaction	radd fi'l (m)	ردّ فعل
risk	muχãṭara (f)	مخاطرة
secret	sirr (m)	سرّ
series	silsila (f)	سلسلة

shape (outer form)	ʃakl (m)	شكل
situation	ḥãla (f), waḍ' (m)	حالة، وضع
solution	ḥall (m)	حلّ
standard (adj)	qiyãsiy	قياسيّ

stop (pause)	istirāḥa (f)	إستراحة
style	uslūb (m)	أسلوب
system	niẓām (m)	نظام
table (chart)	ʒadwal (m)	جدول
tempo, rate	surʿa (f)	سرعة

term (word, expression)	musṭalaḥ (m)	مصطلح
truth (e.g., moment of ~)	ḥaqīqa (f)	حقيقة
turn (please wait your ~)	dawr (m)	دور
urgent (adj)	ʿāʒil	عاجل

utility (usefulness)	manfaʿa (f)	منفعة
variant (alternative)	ʃakl muxtalif (m)	شكل مختلف
way (means, method)	ṭarīqa (f)	طريقة
zone	minṭaqa (f)	منطقة

26. Modifiers. Adjectives. Part 1

additional (adj)	iḍāfiy	إضافيّ
ancient (~ civilization)	qadīm	قديم
artificial (adj)	ṣināʿiy	صناعيّ
bad (adj)	sayyiʼ	سيئ
beautiful (person)	ʒamīl	جميل

big (in size)	kabīr	كبير
bitter (taste)	murr	مرّ
blind (sightless)	aʿma	أعمى
central (adj)	markaziy	مركزيّ

children's (adj)	lil aṭfāl	للأطفال
clandestine (secret)	sirriy	سرّيّ
clean (free from dirt)	naẓīf	نظيف
clever (smart)	ðakiy	ذكيّ
compatible (adj)	mutawāfiq	متوافق

contented (satisfied)	rāḍi	راض
dangerous (adj)	xaṭīr	خطير
dead (not alive)	mayyit	ميّت
dense (fog, smoke)	kaθīf	كثيف
difficult (decision)	ṣaʿb	صعب

dirty (not clean)	wasix	وسخ
easy (not difficult)	sahl	سهل
empty (glass, room)	xāli	خال
exact (amount)	daqīq	دقيق
excellent (adj)	mumtāz	ممتاز

excessive (adj)	mufriṭ	مفرط
exterior (adj)	xāriʒiy	خارجيّ
fast (quick)	sarīʿ	سريع

fertile (land, soil)	χaṣib	خصب
fragile (china, glass)	haʃʃ	هشّ
free (at no cost)	maʒʒāniy	مجّانيّ
fresh (~ water)	ʿaðb	عذب
frozen (food)	muʒammad	مجمّد
full (completely filled)	malyān	مليان
happy (adj)	saʿīd	سعيد
hard (not soft)	ʒāmid	جامد
huge (adj)	ḍaχm	ضخم
ill (sick, unwell)	marīḍ	مريض
immobile (adj)	θābit	ثابت
important (adj)	muhimm	مهمّ
interior (adj)	dāχiliy	داخليّ
last (e.g., ~ week)	māḍi	ماض
last (final)	ʾāχir	آخر
left (e.g., ~ side)	al yasār	اليسار
legal (legitimate)	qānūniy, ʃarʿiy	قانونيّ، شرعيّ
light (in weight)	χafīf	خفيف
liquid (fluid)	sāʾil	سائل
long (e.g., ~ hair)	ṭawīl	طويل
loud (voice, etc.)	ʿāli	عال
low (voice)	munχafiḍ	منخفض

27. Modifiers. Adjectives. Part 2

main (principal)	raʾīsi	رئيسي
matt, matte	munṭafiʾ	منطفئ
mysterious (adj)	γarīb	غريب
narrow (street, etc.)	ḍayyiq	ضيّق
native (~ country)	aṣliy	أصليّ
negative (~ response)	salbiy	سلبيّ
new (adj)	ʒadīd	جديد
next (e.g., ~ week)	muqbil	مقبل
normal (adj)	ʿādiy	عاديّ
not difficult (adj)	γayr ṣaʿb	غير صعب
obligatory (adj)	ḍarūriy	ضروريّ
old (house)	qadīm	قديم
open (adj)	maftūḥ	مفتوح
opposite (adj)	muqābil	مقابل
ordinary (usual)	ʿādiy	عاديّ
original (unusual)	aṣliy	أصليّ
personal (adj)	ʃaχṣiy	شخصيّ
polite (adj)	muʾaddab	مؤدّب

poor (not rich)	faqīr	فقير
possible (adj)	mumkin	ممكن
principal (main)	asāsiy	أساسيّ
probable (adj)	muḥtamal	محتمل
prolonged (e.g., ~ applause)	mumtadd	ممتدّ
public (open to all)	ʿāmm	عامّ
rare (adj)	nādir	نادر
raw (uncooked)	nayy	نيّ
right (not left)	al yamīn	اليمين
ripe (fruit)	nāḍiʒ	ناضج
risky (adj)	χaṭir	خطر
sad (~ look)	ḥazīn	حزين
second hand (adj)	mustaʿmal	مستعمل
shallow (water)	ḍaḥl	ضحل
sharp (blade, etc.)	ḥādd	حادّ
short (in length)	qaṣīr	قصير
similar (adj)	ʃabīh	شبيه
small (in size)	saγīr	صغير
smooth (surface)	amlas	أملس
soft (~ toys)	ṭariy	طريّ
solid (~ wall)	matīn	متين
sour (flavor, taste)	ḥāmiḍ	حامض
spacious (house, etc.)	wāsiʿ	واسع
special (adj)	χāṣṣ	خاصّ
straight (line, road)	mustaqīm	مستقيم
strong (person)	qawiy	قويّ
stupid (foolish)	γabiy	غبيّ
superb, perfect (adj)	mumtāz	ممتاز
sweet (sugary)	musakkar	مسكّر
tan (adj)	asmar	أسمر
tasty (delicious)	laðīð	لذيذ
unclear (adj)	γayr wāḍiḥ	غير واضح

28. Verbs. Part 1

to accuse (vt)	ittaham	إتّهم
to agree (say yes)	ittafaq	إتّفق
to announce (vt)	aʿlan	أعلن
to answer (vi, vt)	aʒāb	أجاب
to apologize (vi)	iʿtaðar	إعتذر
to arrive (vi)	waṣal	وصل
to ask (~ oneself)	sa'al	سأل

to be absent	ɣāb	غاب
to be afraid	χāf	خاف
to be born	wulid	وُلد

to be in a hurry	istaʒal	إستعجل
to beat (to hit)	ḍarab	ضرب
to begin (vt)	bada'	بدأ
to believe (in God)	'āman	آمن
to belong to ...	χaṣṣ	خصّ
to break (split into pieces)	kasar	كسر

to build (vt)	bana	بنى
to buy (purchase)	iʃtara	إشترى
can (v aux)	istaṭā'	إستطاع
can (v aux)	istaṭā'	إستطاع
to cancel (call off)	alɣa	ألغى

to catch (vt)	amsak	أمسك
to change (vt)	ɣayyar	غيّر
to check (to examine)	iχtabar	إختبر
to choose (select)	iχtār	إختار
to clean up (tidy)	rattab	رتّب

to close (vt)	aɣlaq	أغلق
to compare (vt)	qāran	قارن
to complain (vi, vt)	ʃaka	شكا
to confirm (vt)	aθbat	أثبت
to congratulate (vt)	hanna'	هنّأ

to cook (dinner)	ḥaḍḍar	حضّر
to copy (vt)	nasaχ	نسخ
to cost (vt)	kallaf	كلّف
to count (add up)	'add	عدّ
to count on ...	i'tamad 'ala ...	...إعتمد على

to create (vt)	χalaq	خلق
to cry (weep)	baka	بكى
to dance (vi, vt)	raqaṣ	رقص
to deceive (vi, vt)	χada'	خدع
to decide (~ to do sth)	qarrar	قرّر

to delete (vt)	masaḥ	مسح
to demand (request firmly)	ṭālib	طالب
to deny (vt)	ankar	أنكر
to depend on ...	ta'allaq bi ...	...تعلّق بـ
to despise (vt)	iḥtaqar	إحتقر

to die (vi)	māt	مات
to dig (vt)	ḥafar	حفر
to disappear (vi)	iχtafa	إختفى
to discuss (vt)	nāqaʃ	ناقش
to disturb (vt)	az'aʒ	أزعج

29. Verbs. Part 2

to dive (vi)	ɣās	غاص
to divorce (vi)	ṭallaq	طلق
to do (vt)	'amal	عمل
to doubt (have doubts)	ʃakk fi	شك في
to drink (vi, vt)	ʃarib	شرب
to drop (let fall)	awqa'	أوقع
to dry (clothes, hair)	ʒaffaf	جفّف
to eat (vi, vt)	akal	أكل
to end (~ a relationship)	anha	أنهى
to excuse (forgive)	'aðar	عذر
to exist (vi)	kān mawʒūd	كان موجودًا
to expect (foresee)	tanabba'	تنبّأ
to explain (vt)	ʃaraḥ	شرح
to fall (vi)	saqaṭ	سقط
to fight (street fight, etc.)	ta'ārak	تعارك
to find (vt)	waʒad	وجد
to finish (vt)	atamm	أتمّ
to fly (vi)	ṭār	طار
to forbid (vt)	mana'	منع
to forget (vi, vt)	nasiy	نسي
to forgive (vt)	'afa	عفا
to get tired	ta'ib	تعب
to give (vt)	a'ṭa	أعطى
to go (on foot)	maʃa	مشى
to hate (vt)	karah	كره
to have (vt)	malak	ملك
to have breakfast	afṭar	أفطر
to have dinner	ta'aʃʃa	تعشّى
to have lunch	taɣadda	تغدّى
to hear (vt)	sami'	سمع
to help (vt)	sā'ad	ساعد
to hide (vt)	χaba'	خبأ
to hope (vi, vt)	tamanna	تمنّى
to hunt (vi, vt)	iṣṭād	إصطاد
to hurry (vi)	ista'ʒal	إستعجل
to insist (vi, vt)	aṣarr	أصرّ
to insult (vt)	ahān	أهان
to invite (vt)	da'a	دعا
to joke (vi)	mazaḥ	مزح
to keep (vt)	ḥafaẓ	حفظ
to kill (vt)	qatal	قتل
to know (sb)	'araf	عرف

to know (sth)	'araf	عرف
to like (I like ...)	a'ʒab	أعجب
to look at ...	naẓar	نظر
to lose (umbrella, etc.)	faqad	فقد
to love (sb)	aḥabb	أحبَّ
to make a mistake	axṭa'	أخطأ
to meet (vi, vt)	qābal	قابل
to miss (school, etc.)	ɣāb	غاب

30. Verbs. Part 3

to obey (vi, vt)	ṭā'	طاع
to open (vt)	fataḥ	فتح
to participate (vi)	iʃtarak	إشترك
to pay (vi, vt)	dafa'	دفع
to permit (vt)	samaḥ	سمح
to play (children)	la'ib	لعب
to pray (vi, vt)	ṣalla	صلّى
to promise (vt)	wa'ad	وعد
to propose (vt)	iqtaraḥ	إقترح
to prove (vt)	aθbat	أثبت
to read (vi, vt)	qara'	قرأ
to receive (vt)	istalam	إستلم
to rent (sth from sb)	ista'ʒar	إستأجر
to repeat (say again)	karrar	كرّر
to reserve, to book	ḥaʒaz	حجز
to run (vi)	ʒara	جرى
to save (rescue)	anqað	أنقذ
to say (~ thank you)	qāl	قال
to see (vt)	ra'a	رأى
to sell (vt)	bā'	باع
to send (vt)	arsal	أرسل
to shoot (vi)	aṭlaq an nār	أطلق النار
to shout (vi)	ṣarax	صرخ
to show (vt)	'araḍ	عرض
to sign (document)	waqqa'	وقّع
to sing (vi)	ɣanna	غنّى
to sit down (vi)	ʒalas	جلس
to smile (vi)	ibtasam	إبتسم
to speak (vi, vt)	takallam	تكلّم
to steal (money, etc.)	saraq	سرق
to stop (please ~ calling me)	tawaqqaf	توقّف
to study (vt)	daras	درس

to swim (vi)	sabaḥ	سبح
to take (vt)	aχað	أخذ
to talk to …	takallam ma'a …	...تكلّم مع
to tell (story, joke)	ḥaddaθ	حدّث
to thank (vt)	ʃakar	شكر
to think (vi, vt)	ẓann	ظنّ
to translate (vt)	tarʒam	ترجم
to trust (vt)	waθiq	وثق
to try (attempt)	ḥāwal	حاول
to turn (e.g., ~ left)	in'aṭaf	إنعطف
to turn off	ṭaffa	طفى
to turn on	fataḥ, ʃaɣɣal	فتح, شغّل
to understand (vt)	fahim	فهم
to wait (vt)	intaẓar	إنتظر
to want (wish, desire)	arād	أراد
to work (vi)	'amal	عمل
to write (vt)	katab	كتب